Crash Course in Storytelling

Kendall Haven and MaryGay Ducey

Crash Course Series

LIBRARIES
UNLIMITED
A Member of the Greenwood Publishing Group

Westport, Connecticut • London

Library of Congress Cataloging-in-Publication Data

Haven, Kendall F.
  Crash course in storytelling / by Kendall Haven and MaryGay Ducey.
    p. cm. — (Crash course)
  Includes bibliographical references and index.
  ISBN 1-59158-399-3 (pbk : alk. paper)
  1. Storytelling. I. Ducey, MaryGay. II. Title.
  LB1042.H388   2007
  372.67'7—dc22   2006030670

British Library Cataloguing in Publication Data is available.

Library of Congress Catalog Card Number: 2006030670
ISBN: 1-59158-399-3

First published in 2007

Libraries Unlimited, 88 Post Road West, Westport, CT 06881
A Member of the Greenwood Publishing Group, Inc.
www.lu.com

Printed in the United States of America

The paper used in this book complies with the
Permanent Paper Standard issued by the National
Information Standards Organization (Z39.48–1984).

10 9 8 7 6 5 4 3 2 1

This book is dedicated to
Patrick Ducey
Dylan Brie Ducey, and
Patrick Seth Ducey

Contents

INTRODUCTION

"Do you tell stories?" Amazingly, many people answer, "No." Might as well ask, "Do you breathe?" Of course you tell stories. You might think your stories don't compare to the dramatic performances you've seen by famed professional tellers. But so what? Some go so far as to think that their storytelling doesn't count. Not true! Your stories are every bit as legitimate and valuable a part of storytelling and are just as important.

Storytelling is the art of using language, vocalization, and/or physical movement and gesture to reveal the elements and images of a story to a specific, live audience. That's what humans do. Storytelling is as old as the human race and has been a cherished human activity for tens of thousands of years.

Storytelling in the United States survived through the early twentieth century in two places: private homes (where family members told to entertain and to inform family and friends) and public libraries. In the 1970s a new phenomenon emerged: American professional storytelling. These tellers' stories were designed for entertainment; the style quickly became theatrical.

The spread of professional tellers has infused storytelling into the fiber and flow of daily life and has encouraged community organizations and groups to tell more stories and to create more opportunities for storytelling, though (surprisingly—at least to many of us who call ourselves storytellers) not nearly to the extent anticipated or hoped for. It's as if many people now think that storytelling is a special art form that should be practiced only by dedicated, skilled professionals.

Nothing could be further from the truth. Storytelling is a human attribute, a human skill—even a human birthright—that belongs to everyone. Yes, polished, practiced professionals are fun to watch. But that does not diminish the value of, nor the enjoyment others will derive from, the telling you do. In part because libraries have focused on occasional headliner performances by a hired professional, we wonder if these artists have discouraged some library staff members from telling themselves.

We have written this book to pool both our experience in, and our perspective on, storytelling. Gay Ducey is a professional storyteller with twenty-five years' experience who has also served as a children's librarian at the Oakland (California) Public Library for twenty-five years. She brings both an understanding of the interplay of library operations and storytelling and significant insights into the process of telling stories. She has served long and well on all sides of this issue: as the invited professional teller, as the librarian teller, and as the librarian who brings in other professional tellers.

Kendall Haven jumped to storytelling from the world of science. With twenty-five years of experience as a teller and writer working primarily with schools and in the field of education, he brings both practical experience and a penchant for analytical assessment to this writing effort.

Gay and Kendall share the same general philosophy, which permeates this work. Most of what is written here is a melding of our common experiences and beliefs. Where statements reflect the unique experience or belief of one of us, those statements are labeled by name.

Professional storytellers abound in the United States—polished performers working from polished stages to appreciative crowds. However, we believe that professional storytelling is only one end of the continuum of storytelling in a healthy community. There is a vital role to be filled at the community level for stories and storytelling. There is no better nor more logical location to provide this level of storytelling fare than the library. That's YOU, the local librarian. In this book we hope to encourage you to try more storytelling. We hope to gently nudge you to stretch your storytelling wings, to prove to yourself and to your patrons that your storytelling skills are more than equal to the task of providing your community with a steady diet of storytelling.

Storytelling has proven value—to the listeners, to the community, and to the library. This book is our attempt to contribute to elevating the prominence of storytelling in libraries.

This book is not intended to serve as a performance guide for experienced tellers, nor is it primarily a sourcebook for stories to tell. It is a guide to the simplicity and elegance of natural storytelling for those who are not fully convinced of either their storytelling ability or storytelling's place in their library. We have filled this book with tested and proven techniques and ideas for you to use. It represents the wisdom produced from over fifty years of combined storytelling experience.

There is not one "correct" style for storytelling, not one "correct" way to tell a story. Just the opposite. The richness of storytelling depends on each teller finding a style and delivery that feels comfortable and natural. The glory and attraction of storytelling comes from this range and variety. There is room for and need for all styles.

Still, we believe that too few librarians tell stories. Some tell us that they have no time to learn and rehearse stories. Some feel that they simply don't have the ability to do it. Some think it's too hard and prefer to stick to reading. Some believe that storytelling requires a special talent that they may not have.

We don't believe it. By the end of this book, we hope you won't either. Enjoy!

CHAPTER 1

The Place for Storytelling in Your Library

LIBRARIES *ARE* STORIES

Libraries are institutions in service to stories and information. The public library, in particular, is a kind of repository of discourse. Not just in print, either. The library's collections of stories include films, recordings, documents, meetings, talks, local history, genealogy, author visits, programs, and time and space for patrons to simply talk. The library is a place in conversation with the culture at large.

Library staff anchors the institution. Those of us in public service like to share information, impressions, recommendations, and resources. We like to talk to our patrons. Since good conversation is based on constructing a cogent narrative, librarians have more experience in shooting the breeze than those in many other professions. We present programs for all ages, and storytelling fits right into most of them. Just a cursory look at your monthly schedule will reveal the number of hours spent in program presentation, class visits, reference, and outreach.

We often persuade a visitor to try a new title or to tell us what books she or he has been reading. In the course of determining what help is needed we find ourselves listening to a story as it unwinds, and telling one in turn.

A visit to a contemporary public library will soon dispel the stereotype of the sensible-shoed, bun-coiffed, glasses-dangling, middle-aged woman who seems to be protecting the books from the unworthy. Librarians are very savvy about retrieving information from the Internet, gauging the reading level of a silent third grader, finding the right book for the right person at the right time, balancing a budget, stretching resources, and making friends. No wonder we are naturally good at telling tales.

WE'VE BEEN TELLING FOR A LONG TIME

Storytelling has a long, honorable history in the public library. Perhaps the most visible example of that history has involved service to young people. The New York Public Library, for instance, blazed a glorious trail for storytelling decades ago when Ruth Sawyer began the first storytelling program there in 1908. Far from being a glamorous extra, storytelling was an integral service for children. But telling stories is far too much fun, far too valuable, and far too effective to be the prize of the nursery. It belongs to all of us.

Libraries are busy places. The days of a quiet sanctuary for the quiet seeker of knowledge are gone, if they ever existed. Librarians have too much to do, and too little time in which to do it. We know that. We wouldn't suggest another professional investment if we didn't think it would make your work more rewarding, serve your patrons more effectively, and, best of all, be enjoyable.

Storytelling is the most effective educational tool for the least amount of effort. It employs the skills you already possess and puts them to good use. Think of it as another way to meet the mandate of promoting literature and ideas—a really entertaining way. It is also a valuable addition in the effort to encourage literacy for all ages and all cultures.

WHAT KIND OF STORIES?

Storytelling changes the picture. Slipping a told story into a preschool storytime presents literature in a fresh and novel way. It allows for a more engaging presentation for groups visiting the library. The story can be from the great collections of traditional tales that beg to be freed from the book, or an excerpt from chosen fiction or nonfiction. A simple folktale can marry well with books during a program. History can become story and lead listeners to following the path into the past.

That story you tell about your bad grade can showcase books about school or study habits. Your mother's famous piano recital becomes the bridge for a talk about skills, talents, and of course, inevitable failures. An urban legend can open the creaky door of books about mysterious events. Anything will serve. The key is the process of story*telling* as the way you choose to deliver story material to your listeners. Any of these types of stories—or many others—become engaging elements of your program when you *tell* them.

WHAT'S IN IT FOR YOU?

The more you tell stories, the better you tell them. Your professional life will always include presentations, some more challenging than others. Polish up your storytelling skills, find some enriching tales and you will improve your presentational style and confidence.

Not all of those who visit the library are comfortable with print. Some people find the oral approach to literature much easier to absorb and retain. Gay knows this from experience since it was told stories, not print, that her A.D.D. son responded to, whether they were old tales, personal stories, or science tidbits. A good story reached that learner very well since it leveled the cognitive playing field. Or at least minimized the gradation.

Librarianship is one of the few professions in which every single thing you know or have experienced is useful, so your own personal interests, possessions, background become grist for the story mill. You already have a wealth of information to share, and it is easy to convert it into good stories.

Need more? There's nothing like a story to engage and entertain an audience. Your telling brings listeners to you, makes you accessible and approachable. We know how important that is in forging relationships with our patrons. Besides, there's nothing like a professional change of pace to refresh us. Stories of myth, legend, folktale, fairy tale, epic, and fable are the great literary treasure of every culture. As the heirs to that hoard, we can give it to others in the way it deserves to be shared: by telling. (P.S.: you get to keep it, too.)

FROM KITCHEN TABLE TO CARNEGIE HALL: THE THREE LEVELS OF STORYTELLING

Although our evidence is anecdotal, both of us have noticed how few library storytellers we run across in our travels. More often, we (and other professional tellers) are the storytellers, who come in to do a performance or two, gather the glory, and then hit the road. We also know, again anecdotally, that libraries routinely use the services of professional storytellers as entertainers linked to a particular holiday or summer program.

We don't presume to understand all the reasons for this reliance on declared professional tellers. But we have both seen it and become aware of its deleterious impact on a community.

It doesn't have to be that way. It shouldn't be that way. But it is. It may be that library staff see those professional storytellers and think; "I could never, ever do that." "That"—when taken literally—may well be true. You may never, ever become a professional storyteller. But that has nothing to do with your becoming a successful storyteller within the library. The expectations, and performance requirements of a polished professional telling on a raised stage to a thousand listeners are different from those of friends sharing stories around the kitchen table, for instance. Common sense tells us that, but that doesn't mean one is more important than another.

Think of it this way: professional chefs clog the landscape of the Food Network, demonstrating their finesse, their perfect confections, their glib on-air delivery, and their panache. For those who are interested, it is a dazzling display. But we never see them cooking at home, only in the hot lights of a show. Books, CDs, upscale kitchen ware all bear the name of The Famous Chef. Many a cook has learned a good deal by watching these pros work and been inspired to try a dish or two. That's what they do best: inspire, motivate, entertain. The food is fancy, and it would be great to sit down to the table for such a meal once in a long while.

Most of us who like to cook on occasion, and even those who cook every day, are not going to become Iron Chefs and will never challenge Emeril for his primetime TV slot. Yet we can whip up an appetizing dinner that will please—even thrill—our families more often than not, and sometimes we can mount a holiday dinner that confounds even our mothers-in-law. Storytelling is like that. It has room for everyone who wants to tell a tale. It is not confined to those who choose to make a living at it.

Granted, some folks have a gift. We readily admit that. They are uncommonly talented. But just as you would not stop cooking because you haven't been picked up for a pilot, so, too, you should not avoid telling stories just because there are some storytellers who are better than you believe yourself to be. That would be a shame, for you would deny the gifts of story literature to the children and adults who patronize your library, except on those few, scattered occasions when the hired narrative gun sweeps into town. That's not enough.

We offer the following idea: storytelling has levels. None is more important than another, but they differ, so it is helpful to distinguish between them.

Level 1: The Informal Storyteller

Informal storytelling happens throughout the routine course of our daily lives. Occasionally planned but more often spontaneous, conversational, and interactive in nature, informal storytelling forms an essential part of the fabric of our normal communications. Stories told across the family dinner table, by the auto mechanic running your smog check, in the supermarket checkout line, during chance meetings of friends and colleagues—these are all times when we automatically slip into the role of informal storytellers.

We don't usually plan or organize the text, nor do we practice or try to refine our style or voices. Some of the stories are brand new, the stuff of the day; others are well-worn narratives about our families that each member knows by heart. Around the kitchen table, these stories ebb and flow, sometimes punctuated by someone else adding a detail or correction. Above all, informal storytelling is a natural and unrehearsed part of human communications.

Level 2: The Community Storyteller

This sort of storytelling usually takes place within the professional setting. The library, the classroom, the pulpit, the courtroom, each of these is the native habitat for tales. In ancient times, the storyteller passed on stories of wisdom and heritage. The tales reflected the prevailing values and exposed new listeners to important information that kept them safe and taught them how to behave. Adults heard the stories that glorified the community's valorous history, or traced lineage. Novelty was not useful. Continuity was essential.

Contemporary visitors to the library need and deserve these stories still. This is the setting in which the children and adults can hear stories that feed the soul and free the imagination. It is desirable for the storyteller to be familiar, and the stories, too. At this level, stories can and should be repeated again and again. Community storytellers do not need to perform. They need to share. The style of the storyteller is unimportant. From a very dramatic teller to one who has a quiet, intimate approach, each is useful.

Level 3: The Professional Storyteller

The professional storyteller delivers a polished, rehearsed performance, usually to a relatively large audience. It is not uncommon for the performance to have a title. The storyteller may well be traveling through, never to be seen again. Styles may differ, but the teller is often larger than life and the performance is formally staged. Our expectations are high; we anticipate seeing a well-prepared artist with strong, precise language and physical preparation. Level 3 is something like a holiday feast, a rare, rich treat, to be enjoyed occasionally, not as a steady diet. We all benefit from these occasional storytellers, but the place for day-in and day-out storytelling is with you, the library storyteller.

It was when we started to use professional storytellers as the primary designated artistic hitters that we got off track. Libraries can facilitate all three levels of storytelling. Encourage and facilitate informal telling. Arrange and sponsor occasional professional performances.

And accept your role as a primary provider of a steady diet of community level storytelling.

THE PLACE FOR STORYTELLING IN YOUR LIBRARY

Many opportunities for storytelling exist in your library. This list of five is not intended to be exhaustive; rather, it represents proven niches for your storytelling. Let these ideas free you to identify the many other ways you can weave storytelling into your library and programs.

1. As a snazzy addition to preschool and early elementary storytimes.

2. As an effective, natural, direct form of booktalking. And not just for audiences of elementary school children. When presenting "booktalks" to middle and high school audiences, stories (riddling tales, urban legends, brief information about a famous guy) can be effectively incorporated into presentations (see Gail de Vos's book about storytelling for teens in the Bibliography). As an alternative to the normal booktalk fare for longer books (telling a little bit about the book, main character, and/or author but not the end), consider taking one incident within the book and simply tell the whole thing.

3. As an evening performance for families and older kids. Granted, these performances often feature the storyteller-for-hire. Let's change that. Once you have a few tales under your belt, you can at least complement the guest performer, or, better, start offering programs featuring YOU (the storyteller).

4. As a special holiday program. You need not do the whole thing. Try combining your talents with several other staff persons, and, like Mickey Rooney and Judy Garland, "put on a show."

5. As part of presentations to community groups or other organizations. Any story that complements your presentation will be well received by the audience. Try a fable, a story about Mullah Nasruddin, or any short tale that suits you and the occasion. Emphasis is on brief, fast, and either amusing or thoughtful, whichever the context suggests.

So let's take it back. Let's claim storytelling as a valuable offering to our constituents. And let's do it ourselves.

CHAPTER 2

Why Tell It?: The Power of Storytelling

Chapter 1 described a role for the different levels of storytelling as integral parts of your library programs. That chapter showed what storytelling can do for your library programs. There are eight additional reasons for *you* to tell stories as an important part of your library's offerings. We know that most of you already view storytelling as valuable and worthwhile and may not need new evidence of its power and value. Consider this list a gentle reminder of how important you and your telling are in the lives and development of your young patrons and what a gift your storytelling can be.

BECAUSE YOU *CAN*

As you'll see throughout this book, you already know most of what you'll need to know, and have the innate talent you'll need, to tell stories successfully and effectively.

BECAUSE LIBRARY PATRONS NEED YOUR STORIES

Everyone benefits from listening to stories being told: traditional tales, folktales, "Just So" stories, myths, etc. We all need to hear these stories being told with enthusiasm, and need to absorb the form, patterns, rhythms, and content of these stories.

Children especially need the developmental benefits of hearing complete stories being told, and they need the cognitive value woven into the content of these stories that have been honed and refined over countless generations of successful tellings by countless tellers. For many children *you* are a primary source of this level of storytelling. They depend on you. They need you. Their development depends, in a small but real part, on the story and storytelling exposure you provide.

A Canadian study published in 2004 (O'Neill, Pearce, and Pick, 2004) studied the storytelling ability of preschool children in Ontario, Canada, and found good correlation between early storytelling skills and later math abilities. They suggest that time spent telling stories to children and allowing them to informally and improvisationally tell stories to develop their own storytelling skill during preschool years is likely to improve math skill upon entering school.

More important than its specific focus on math skills, this study establishes storytelling skill (structural knowledge and story map thinking) as predating, and as a precursor for, the development of logical thinking. Cognitive science studies have confirmed that human beings develop the ability to understand and interpret the world around them through story structure and story concepts long before they develop logical thinking (see Appendix 2). In fact, logical thinking seems to evolve out of story structural thinking. The ability to interpret experiences and to create meaning using story thinking comes from exposure to stories during the early formative years. They need your stories.

BECAUSE STORYTELLING IS A GREAT CHANGE OF PACE

Even the best pitchers need to change their pitches unless they want to spend a lot of time on the bench. Break it up. Change the pattern of your programs. If your normal pattern is to *read* stories, storytelling (whether improvisational, informal, or planned) will surprise your listeners and create extra interest.

BECAUSE STORYTELLING IS AFFECTING AND ENGAGING FOR THE AUDIENCE

As a fledgling storyteller, Kendall told stories at an Orange County, California, school—just over a year after he first performed there. As he entered the building, a second-grade girl passed him in the hall and said, "I remember you. You told us stories last year."

Then that seven-year-old girl began to tell the stories she had heard a year before. They were original stories and she had only heard them once. Still, a year later, both stories tumbled out of her, vividly and accurately, with no prompting. That is not at all unusual. Virtually ever storyteller in the country has had this experience. Stories deeply engage and entrance an audience.

Don't worry. Just because there are professional storytellers out there who visit the public library and wow the crowds does not mean they have a life lease on this captivating experience. Gay tells stories in the library as well as telling stories as a professional. Recently a fifth grader returned to the branch after a long absence. "Do you still tell that story about the sultan, the little rooster and the diamond button?" he asked. "Yes" she said "Just this week. Is it one of your favorites?" "Yes" he said, as he began to tell it back to her. It happens all the time and to *everyone* who regularly tells stories. It is inherent in the *process* of storytelling, not in some unique property of skilled and theatrical performers.

Brain research confirms what storytellers know from experience. Bransford and Brown (2000), Engle (1995), Fisher (1994), Bruner (1990), and other neuroscientists have studied this phenomenon and have drawn two general conclusions:

1. Evolution has "hardwired" the process and form of storytelling into human brains and minds. Fisher concludes that humans are really *homo narratus,* and that storytelling is an intrinsic human attribute. That is, story architecture is hardwired into the human mind. Bruner has observed that storytelling predates written communication by 50,000 years and that the form and pattern of storytelling are now, as it were,

residue of many thousands of years of evolutionary programming.

2. We learn through storytelling. We learn the pattern, rhythm, and structure of oral storytelling long before we learn the rhythms and patterns of written stories. Young infants learn to pay attention to the features of oral speech (such as intonation and rhythm) that help them obtain critical information about language and meaning.

Perhaps we respond so positively and powerfully to storytelling because we are genetically predisposed to favor the form. That's certainly what we think. Your listeners will be more responsive to your *storytelling* than to the same story delivered in other ways.

BECAUSE STORYTELLING MAKES NONFICTION EVENTS AND TOPICS COME ALIVE

Dan Fossler, a California high school music teacher, took a storytelling course and created a story about the Italian composer, Vivaldi, for his final exercise. The story was a rousing hit. So he told it to his student orchestra the next fall before assigning them a Vivaldi piece. He was amazed at how quickly this orchestra mastered the difficult piece.

He scanned their home practice logs and found that this group was practicing an average of 20 percent more on this piece than had his previous orchestras. When he asked them why, they reported that Vivaldi was "cool" and that they liked him and his music. Ten students had gone to the library to check out additional reading material on Vivaldi. In short, Fossler's told story made Vivaldi real, accessible and interesting. It created context and relevance. Storytelling does that.

Librarians have booktalked for years, just as Mr. Fossler did, using episodes from the lives of the famous and not so famous to entice listeners into reading more. It's storytelling, really, and it works. Any topic can be introduced to listeners through a tale. Brief folktales can introduce the sciences; personal stories can be woven into sports and the arts; and the 900s offer opportunities for folktales, myths, legends . . . just about any sort of story.

BECAUSE STORYTELLING GENERATES VIVID AND DETAILED IMAGES IN A LISTENER'S MIND

Kendall once conducted an experiment with primary students in eight schools (total of 1,090 students and six performances). During short assemblies, he told one story and read a different story of about the same length. Students returned to the classroom and, with no discussion, each drew one picture from just one of the two stories. He varied both the order and the specific stories he presented. But the variations never affected the final results. Between 78 and 86 percent in each class drew a picture of the story that was told. Storytelling seems to create stronger, more vivid and more memorable imagery.

When being read a picture book, young listeners almost always ask to see the pictures. But when a story is being told, listeners have no need for pictures. Listening encourages them to create their own images, tailor-made to suit each child.

Recent neurological research has shown that memory depends on the density of sensory details associated with the event. The greater the number of sensory details filed away into memory surrounding an event or idea, the easier and more likely it is that a person will recall that event or idea.

Listening to stories creates vivid, multisensory details. Details create memory.

BECAUSE STORYTELLING HELPS THOSE WHO STRUGGLE WITH LANGUAGE TO UNDERSTAND AND INTERPRET THE STORY

When reading a book, you use vocal tools, such as tone, pace, and volume to interpret the text. Storytelling does that too. But storytelling more readily allows for physical interpretation of the story through gesture, movement, and expression. These interpretations can vary from dancing across the floor to the most subtle body language. And they are effective in aiding listeners to interpret and visualize the story.

Improvisation is a natural part of storytelling. Tellers refine or change their language and delivery in response to the audience reaction. Although small text changes are possible when reading, readers strive to stick closely to the author's words.

Cooper (1997) conducted an extensive study of how in-class storytelling affects students' development of the ability to extract meaning from texts. He concluded, first, that storytelling significantly enhanced students' understanding of story text and, second, that a major part of this enhancement came from the improvisational nature of storytelling that allowed the teller to acknowledge and respond to student verbal and nonverbal responses and to adjust the telling to incorporate those responses. Students' ability to interact with the teller and to have the teller adjust the story and the telling to account for those responses significantly improved students' ability to understand stories and to create meaning from stories.

BECAUSE STORYTELLING CONNECTS LISTENERS TO *YOU*

To many patrons, *you* are the library. Storytelling can strengthen that impression. It forges an intimate relationship between teller and listener that continues far beyond the actual telling of a tale. It doesn't really matter what kind of story you tell, where you tell it, or what kind of event it is. It might be part of a planned, formal program, or an improvisational, off-the-cuff story about your family or your own experiences. Regardless of what you choose to tell, the story works to creates the bond. It is always a shared experience.

So, why storytelling? Because it produces all of the results—the topical and general interest, the delight, the engagement, the entertainment, and the fun—that mark a good presentation.

CHAPTER 3

"Okay, But Can / Really Do It?" Making Storytelling Practical and Doable

ASKING THE RIGHT QUESTION

Storytelling is not a new set of performance skills to learn. It's not about rules. Storytelling is a natural process that we all do, but do automatically (unconsciously) rather than consciously.

During workshops we often ask groups, "Do *you* tell stories?" Many, envisioning a long list of rules and mandates for how one is *supposed* to tell a story, answer "No."

Such people search for the wrong kind of rules to guide them to better, easier storytelling. Should stories be told word for word? Should you use gestures when you tell? Should you move or stand still? Stand or sit? Should you use vocal characterizations? Physical characterizations?

Should stories be told in the third person? In the first? Should stories be presented in chronological order? Should you avoid costumes and props? Name any aspect of storytelling organization and performance that would seem suitable for such a "rule" and you will find successful, respected storytellers who intentionally and successfully violate whatever rule you create.

Those are the wrong kinds of questions to ask and the wrong kinds of "rules" to search for. You don't think about rules when you tell informal stories to your friends and families. You simply tell the story—and usually do just fine.

But there *are* guidelines—actually, more like natural laws—which, like a lighthouse beacon, can serve to guide every teller around the shoals and eddies of storytelling distress. We call them natural laws because, like the law of gravity, they do not tell you what you *should* do (as a speed limit law does), but rather they describe the way the process naturally works. From these natural laws we derive insights and understandings that, like effective rules, guide us to more consistently successful storytelling.

In the mid-1990s the National Storytelling Association spent two years crafting their definition of storytelling. In one sentence, they said: "Storytelling is the art of using language, vocalization, and/or physical movement and gesture to reveal the elements and images of a story to a specific, live audience."

That's storytelling—and that's what we all do every time we share a story with a friend, weave a story into a lecture, or try to entertain sixty fourth graders during a class visit to the library. You already do it.

Asking, "Do you tell?" (or "Do *I* tell?") is the wrong question. The question is as meaningless as asking, "Do you breathe?" We *all* tell stories—personal day-to-day stories—every day. You've told stories virtually every day since you were three years old. That's what humans do.

After quick reflection, many think that a better question to ask is, "Do you tell your stories *well*?" Occasionally, everyone does a lousy job of telling a story. It falls flat; it doesn't work. We've all been cornered at an office party, a family function, or at a reunion by someone who droned through endless and painfully boring stories—Uncle Philbert's trip to the Little League Hall of Fame, Aunt Penny's mortification at being 30¢ short at the check out, a classmate's intriguing life as the third assistant vice president of marketing. We've even done it ourselves.

Again, it's a meaningless question. We guarantee that every reader of this book at *some* time, in *some* place has told at least *one* delightfully mesmerizing, enchanting, totally effective story. Maybe it was only to three of your best friends or two coworkers at the water cooler. Perhaps you've felt really "on," with your listeners eagerly hanging on every word, only a few times in your life. The point is, we guarantee it *has happened*. You have and can tell your stories well. As a community level storyteller, that's all the proof you'll ever need.

What's a better question to ask? Remember our cooking metaphor from Chapter 1? The right question to ask is: Am I trying to be picked for a theatrical TV cooking show that has to wow and entertain a large audience, or am I trying to provide a nutritious and flavorful meal that my family will enjoy? These two types of cooking have radically different mandates and expectations. Which are you trying to do with your storytelling? You're going to be a community level storyteller, so the answer is: cook a nutritious and tasty meal for your listeners. That's very different from becoming an Iron Chef on the Food channel.

The trick for *your* kind of telling—though it's not much of a trick—is simply to know your storytelling self: how you naturally learn, remember, and tell your own stories.

YOU DON'T HAVE TO GET IT RIGHT TO GET IT RIGHT

You see a professional teller and think that every gesture, every pause, every glance, word and tone were perfect. You think, "Wow. She got it right! *That's* what storytelling is supposed to look like."

No. That's what theatrical-main-stage-telling-in-front-of-a-large-audience-of-strangers-in-a-formal-setting-by-*that*-teller is supposed to look like. If that same teller sat in a circle of ten first graders and told the same story in exactly the same way, it would not look or sound nearly as "perfect." It wouldn't even look appropriate. It would look and feel wrong. Why? That style of storytelling is appropriate for one kind of storyteller and one kind of event.

Do you stop a friend in mid-story and refuse to listen any further because she didn't get the words right? Do you feel cheated because you suspect she missed a word? We have yet to meet the person who could honestly answer yes to either question.

Recent neurological research has shown that we humans remember the *gist*, not the specific wording, when we listen to a story. (See Appendix 2 for a summary of relevant research.) Every time neurologists conduct this test, subjects *think* they accurately remember the words. But the words they "remember" are largely their own creation and not in the original text. We humans remember the gist—the idea and the emotion and the meaning of a told story. Then we reinvent our own words to describe what we interpreted and remembered from the story.

Getting a story "right" has to be measured by the images lodged in listeners' minds and by listeners' reactions to the story. Storytelling is not a *verbatim* recitation. It doesn't require you to get the words right. It does require that you get the *gist* of the story right. Luckily, that's much easier and more natural. The gist includes the main flow of events (the plot), the characters and their goals and struggles, and the emotional flow or mood of the story. That is what you are used to learning and telling for your own stories.

"Getting it right" for you will mean just two things: (1) get the story characters and events (sequences) across to your listeners, and (2) tell it in such a way that your natural enthusiasm and passion for the story shines through in your telling. *That* kind of "getting it right" is much easier and more natural and is what your listeners need when you tell.

HOW DO YOU NATURALLY LEARN, RECALL, AND TELL YOUR OWN STORIES?

Sure, you tell stories—anecdotes, incidents, memories of your past, family stories. But you don't consciously think about how you'll tell those informal stories, or how you'll word and structure them. You just tell them. It's like many other unconscious, automatic things you do. You know how to tie shoelaces. But it would be extremely difficult to write down what you do with each thumb and finger in temporal sequential order to get those laces tied. You do it, but don't consciously know how you do it.

We tell stories the same way. We do it, but don't consciously pause to think about *how* we do it. The difference is that if you suddenly doubt your ability to tie shoelaces you need only glance down at your feet to see proof. The problem is that we have no such ready source of proof to remind ourselves of our natural storytelling ability.

The key there is that you do it, and, thus, that you know how to do it. You just have to become a bit more aware of what you already know and naturally do every day.

Recall something that happened to you years ago—some memory, maybe some special event. What popped back up into your conscious mind? Typically, two things appear from your long-term memory when you recall a past event: sensory details (sights, sounds, smells, feels, or tastes) and a memory of the way you felt when it happened. That's what we humans remember efficiently. Cognitive science research has repeatedly confirmed it. We record sensory data. And we record our emotional state to match those sensory impressions.

As most tellers tell the story, something akin to a slide show flashes through their minds as image after image of these sensory details shines onto their mental screens. That's how you typically tell your own stories. Nothing complicated; nothing needing extensive rehearsal or choreography. It's simple, natural storytelling.

Storytelling is supposed to be natural and fun. Telling stories is something we spontaneously burst into when we are having a good time with friends, family, or coworkers. With just a bit of forethought, the same core skills can carry you through more formal library telling. You want to keep the natural storytelling style and system you already successfully use for *all stories* regardless of the source—because that is what already works for you. Don't adjust *you* to fit the story, adjust (or select) *stories* to fit you.

Storytelling is not acting. It is not about mimicking the performances of others. It is not about dramatic theatrics (unless they are natural and comfortable for you). You don't worry about such things when telling your daily-event stories to friends and family members. So don't try to force yourself to worry about them for other stories.

WHAT LISTENERS *REALLY* NEED

Have you ever thought about what listeners need—really *need*—from you when you tell a story? Have you ever wondered what your listeners *don't* absolutely need from your stories? Probably not—and the stories worked just fine. But isn't that a big part of storytelling—to give an audience what it needs—and just what it needs—so that they can conjure vivid, intriguing images in their minds?

There is a game Kendall uses during workshops called *What Makes It Real*. It's the storytelling version of *To Tell the Truth*. He has three people stand and tell a short story that they have discussed and practiced for only ninety seconds. One of them is telling the truth. (It happened to that person.) The other two claim it happened to them. They tell it as if it happened to them. But it didn't. The audience must vote for which story they think is the real version of this story.

It's fun. But its value comes in discussing why people voted as they did. What made one story sound more real than the other two? All mention the same few factors that influenced their votes.

What listeners say they need from the content of the story:

- Appropriate and arresting details

- Relevant, interesting characters

- Intriguing story problem, tension, and suspense (often mentioned under their catch-all synonym "excitement")

- Humor

- Information and concision

- Believability

What listeners say they need from the performance of the story:

- Confidence

- Emotional expression

- Enthusiasm

- Energy

- Humor

Notice what's *not* on this list. No one has ever voted for a story because the teller got all the words right. No one has ever mentioned voting because of the story's action (the sequence of events in the story).

Look at the five items listed in the second half of the list. They all refer to listeners' perceptions of *how* the teller told the story. The listed items refer not directly to what the teller did (use of gestures, facial expression, vocal pacing, etc.), but to the listeners' interpretation of what the teller did. Really, they are all different expressions of a central need of every listener. If listeners believe that the teller believes in the story, then they, too, will believe.

How do listeners decide if they think that a teller likes and is excited by his or her own story? By the *way* the teller said it. Does the teller appear confident, comfortable, and natural? Does the teller appear to be enjoying his or her own story?

Again, this is good news. You are used to pouring your natural enthusiasm into the booktalks you present. You are already skilled in making your listeners see that you enjoy the books you present and describe. Those same skills will serve you well as you begin to tell stories.

THE DIFFERENCE BETWEEN
READING AND TELLING

Librarians, particularly those working with young people, are skilled at reading aloud. They know well the difference between reading a story and listening to a storyteller tell a story. However, there are subtle differences between listening to a story being *read* and listening to a story being *told*. It is worthwhile to review these differences as you decide the role of storytelling in your presentation repertoire.

1. Reading places the book between you and your listeners. Even if you are a skilled reader, the book is still primary to your listeners: the images handed to them rather than created in their minds, the words predetermined.

2. The presence of the book limits your gestures and movements.

3. Reading preserves the author's exact words. Storytelling does not.

4. Reading gives listeners exposure to exceptionally good writing and, in picture books, to exceptionally good illustration.

5. Reading does not require the reader to learn the story.

6. Shifting from reading to telling represents a change of media. Changing the media of delivery changes the expectations (conscious and unconscious) of the listener. As an example, Jack Hitt, a senior editor for *Harpers* magazine in the early 1990s, came to a national storytelling festival and, dazzled by the delight and power of storytelling, decided to print a series of stories in *Harpers* by modern storytellers. He put out a call for tellers who wrote their own stories to submit their favorites for his consideration. He told Kendall that he received 176 submissions (including four from Kendall). Yet he found one—just one—that he believed worked in print, even though he could see how most would be delightful and successful performance pieces. He read the stories out loud to coworkers, who agreed that they would love to hear and see the stories being told, but that they didn't work coming off the printed page. Jack canceled the project. The stories were written and structured for live storytelling and could not survive a shift to the printed page—even when read aloud from that page. When you change media, you change the expectations of the listeners.

Whether reading a story or telling it is right for you will vary from situation to situation and story to story. The more you try story*telling*, the more you will expand the situations in which you feel comfortable telling as opposed to reading. We both believe that telling is a powerful and attractive choice for sharing story material. We also believe that you, as a trained member of the library staff, are better equipped and better able to successfully tell stories than you might think. We are completely convinced that, if you try telling stories, you'll find both that your listeners will overwhelmingly enjoy and appreciate your telling and that your storytelling will be more successful than you imagined.

CHAPTER 4

Choosing Stories That Will Work for *You*

WHERE DO I START?

Start with yourself. After all, you're the one who will be telling the story. The conventional advice is to choose stories that you love. Strong words, and perhaps a bit romantic for some, but it makes sense, because some stories just seem to jump right into your arms and say, "It's me! I'm the one you want."

We find it more accurate to say that you should choose stories that you can't seem to forget, that stay with you, that you instinctively want to tell. What makes one story appealing, and not another, is an artistic mystery. Librarians are familiar with that sort of mystery, because we know that of the ten titles we might toss out to a patron, only one or two make the cut.

WHICH STORIES TO START WITH?

Consider getting used to the *process* of telling stories by telling the easiest stories of all—your own. Slide into it. Tell personal, relevant bits and stories between other material or to introduce other presentations. Experiment with personal stories to see what feels comfortable when you don't have a book in your hand.

You don't have to start by formally telling your listeners that you're going to tell a story. You don't even have to tell complete stories. Start with the simple bits you might tell a friend or family member. Watch what happens as you slip these into your programs. What do you like about these story bits? To what kind of material do you naturally gravitate? What produces the best audience response for you.?

In this way you can use your own stories to gain a better sense of what kinds of stories you want to tell and that will likely work well for you. It's a nice, but not essential, guide to picking stories.

This advice is time-tested and works well for most tellers. For most, but not for all. We recommend that you give it a try. We all come equipped with interesting moments that can be shaped into stories. However, if the mere thought of dragging your personal stories out for public display stabs icicles of fear into your heart, don't force yourself.

HOW TO PICK A STORY

The language in stories gets some storytellers' attention. Others like an unexpected ending. Still others enjoy telling stories from a specific culture, theme, or topic—about tricksters, for instance. As you start to collect and tell tales you may see some commonality between your selections. Storytellers develop an affinity for genre as well, and so become well known for tall tales or ghost stories. In the beginning try lots of stories on and see how they feel. As you develop your story ears and personal style of telling you may settle into a predictable series of stories. That is the time to shop around for new kinds of stories you haven't tried before. Stretching your repertoire is good for your telling.

The past thirty-five years have been busy in storytelling. Some have referred to this period as a storytelling renaissance. Maybe, although the stories were there all along. This upsurge has been responsible for the startling increase of storytelling performance, and the development of storytelling events and festivals, as well as classes. The blessing is that you have chosen to explore storytelling at a time rich in resources. New collections of tales, advice and how-to manuals, and even precise instruction about using stories within particular groups or settings are available for borrowing. You might as well take advantage of this largesse. There are reliable lists of stories for particular age groups and settings that do the work of searching for you.

While nothing replaces the excitement of finding an unknown tale and making it your own, there is a lot to be said for starting with what is tried, true, and available as you begin your journey. You will find stories that are recommended so often it would be folly to ignore them, whether you end up using them or not.

Most of the tales you choose will come to you through reading. The library has such a wealth of traditional tales that you can hardly exhaust it. But it is also important to listen, to train your ears to recognize a good story. The library's audio collection can afford you the luxury of listening to gifted tellers while driving to work. That's good company to keep. Seek out storytelling in your area and make a point of attending events as often as you can. You may know of librarians who tell stories, or it may take a bit of sleuthing to find them. It is particularly important to hear these storytellers, as their styles may differ from those of professional tellers. Professional or not, there is no substitute for being present when a fine tale is shared by a fine storyteller. After a time you will be able to spot the tellable tale very quickly and, just as quickly, know whether it is one you are interested in telling.

WHAT *IS* A STORY?

In the end, you'll choose what pleases you. We know that. But will those stories please your listeners? No way to know for sure, except to try them out.

We have found that information on the elements of a story sharpens your selection skills. A story is a unique and specific narrative that includes a clear plot, at least one character with which the listener can identify, sometimes an antagonist, a problem or conflict to be resolved, a resolution, and a satisfying ending.

Stories containing these informational elements both satisfy, and resonate with, listeners. Traditional tales pass on wisdom, experience, information, and fact, and reinforce prevailing beliefs and values. New stories, fictional or familial, shape beliefs and values. Stories are the building blocks of knowledge, the foundation of collective memory and learning. Stories model effective use of language. Stories encourage empathy and connect us with the best and worst parts of humanity. Stories link past, present, and future and teach us the possible future consequences of our present actions, if we choose to heed them.

There is much of interest and value that we could say about story structure. Entire books have been devoted to the subject. (See Haven, 2004 as an example.) Here, our focus is on *telling* stories, so we have moved our brief discussion of these structural elements into Appendix 1. It is a quick summary of these elements and of their function and contribution to a story and to listeners' appreciation of a story. This appendix isn't essential reading since you won't, as a rule, create your own stories. But it will help you understand the stories you select and tell. It also serves as a handy reference tool to answer questions that might arise as you select, learn, and tell stories. Why is the story organized as it is? Which aspects of the story are most critical to listeners? What can I change (shorten or reorder) without altering the story in a negative way?

WHAT TO LOOK FOR IN A STORY

Once you get a sense of how a story works, and why, you've gone a long way toward making good choices. Each story has a structure. The structure may vary depending on the story type, but in the main, traditional tales depend on a strong plot and a good deal of action. Characters move the plot along and provide someone to cheer or to vilify. Sensory details are limited to the bare essentials in folk material for several reasons. Traditional stories come from specific cultures. Those within the culture didn't need topographical details, or descriptions of clothing and such. The shared knowledge of the community made these unnecessary.

As stories travel about, the sense of place becomes blurred and the story changes with every telling. In transit, stories may have picked up more descriptive material than they started with. That's natural. But this means that it is important to pay attention to the cultural markers within the story that seem to have survived the trip and to live with them for a while before changing them. You are, after all, borrowing something of value, and in doing so it will take on the coloration of your own telling, You cannot freeze the tale like a fly in amber, but you can become familiar enough with the cultural details to do them justice.

With the rise of a professional class of storytellers has come a good deal of discussion of cultural appropriation. Should storytellers recount stories from cultures they don't belong to? Who owns a story? What is the right thing to do? This is a complex topic, but we encourage library storytellers to tell what they wish. You are sharing literature in an oral form, and that's part of your mission. Choose stories carefully, treat them with respect, tell them with joy. In doing so, you honor all traditions.

EVALUATING A STORY

As a summary, here are considerations that the collective experiences of many tellers have shown will guide you toward stories that will be easier for you to learn and more fun for you to tell:

1. Pick stories you like and that you can easily and clearly see in your mind. Did the story grab your interest and attention on first hearing (or reading)? Do you find yourself thinking about the story? Reliving it? Do you like the story well enough to want to learn it?

2. A story with fewer characters is easier. Every extra character adds extra work for you and makes the story more complicated to tell.

3. Short is easier. Short stories have less story to learn and remember. Even in two-minute quickies listeners will still want interesting characters with strong intents, danger-filled obstacles, struggles, and details. They just come faster and with less development in such a short story.

4. Pick stories with a clear plot (sequence of events). Stories with definite, sharp scene breaks are easier to learn than stories in one, continuous flowing sequence.

5. Can you clearly see the structural elements in this story? If you are unclear about them, your listeners will likely be unclear as well.

6. Stories with characters you clearly see and understand in your heart are easier for you to learn and tell. Do you clearly understand the characters' feelings, reactions, goals, and motives? Would you feel comfortable portraying them to an audience?

7. Choose stories with language you don't feel you have to repeat exactly as it appears in the book. Such stories are good candidates for story reading. Good stories to tell are ones that let you comfortably use your own natural vocabulary, phrasing, and manner of talking.

8. Consider stories your audience already knows (or have at least heard before). This is particularly true for young children. If they have heard the story before, they can help you tell it if you ever need or want their participation and assistance.

9. Pick stories that fit with your natural storytelling style and strengths. If, for example, the story is a raucous farce full of physical comedy and you are a quiet teller, this will be a challenge for you to tell.

10. Pick stories that will be appropriate for, relevant to, and interesting to your intended audience. Are these characters, the character information (traits) included in the story, the characters' goals and motives, and the obstacles they face suited for the audience you will face?

You may have already noticed that folktales tend to meet more of these criteria than do any other kinds of stories. You certainly don't have to start with folktales. But they are a consistently reliable source of tellable tales.

Above all else, start with something that feels easy, something enjoyable, something you like. You might want to start with a story you have often read aloud and already know. The more clearly you can see the story start-to-finish in your mind, the faster and easier it will be to learn. After you have told a few stories you picked because they were easy to learn and tell, you'll have the telling experience under your belt to move on to broader story vistas. Let your early experience guide you.

CHAPTER 5

Learning the Stories You Tell

"LEARNING" YOUR OWN STORIES

The best way to start is by doing. Grab a story you know fairly well and try telling it. Don't make it a big production. Just tell it. See how it feels. See where you felt comfortable and strong. See where you felt less sure. Try it a few more times and see what happens. Did your telling change? Were you more confident or less? Did you forget parts? Was it fun? Whatever happened, pat yourself on the back. You're well on the way now.

Although it is more than likely that traditional material will be your mainstay, you can learn a lot by looking at the way you tell your own stories and those of your family. We've said that you already know what you'll need to know to tell stories. So how does that apply to learning a story? Let's start with your own stories. How do you learn stories that happen to you?

Don't say, "I don't have to learn them. They happened to me." After the experience, you had to interpret the events and create a mental stream of information that you transferred to long-term storage (memory) with tags that you could access to recall the event. When you tell these personal stories, you pull *something* out of memory into your conscious brain that directs what you say and how you say it.

Try it. Recall a story (or incident) that happened to you when you were a child. Quickly tell it to someone, anyone. What popped back into your mind? What did you remember?

Most likely you remembered sights, sounds, smells, etc. (sensory images) and how you felt. Remember that from Chapter 3? Filing those impressions into your long-term memory *is* learning the story. Recalling them and converting them into language and gesture *is* remembering. You naturally do it all the time.

That's learning and remembering.

KEEP IT SIMPLE

Advice about learning stories is thick on the ground. Each book or article dutifully lists techniques and suggestions. The remarkable part is the spectrum. On one end are the simplest of suggestions, and on the other end are processes and approaches so labor intensive, so detailed that the reader droops in exhaustion before even beginning. The latter resemble the wrinkled instructions that come with the piece of furniture described as "some assembly needed." You'd have to quit your day job to do this stuff.

Librarians are busy, so let's keep it simple. Try this list of suggestions that many storytellers agree are helpful. They are ubiquitous—because they mostly work. If they work for you and you find you successfully master the tales you want to tell, great! If not, we have included additional techniques—more extensive, but also tested, proven, and reliable—that will serve your needs.

We have split the process of learning stories in half. This first half (Chapter 5) describes the process of initially bringing the story into your mind and heart so that you will be ready for the second half, learning how to get it back out again when you tell. That half is discussed in Chapter 7.

Here is our list of simple learning ideas:

1. **Don't memorize the story—unless it's a literary tale.** (See Chapter 6.) Many hear that advice and nod in agreement, only to then secretly memorize the story for fear that they'll never tell it if they don't. The temptation to memorize is strong in many beginning tellers. Resist the urge! For those who need a bit more on this critical topic, we have included an expanded list or reasons not to memorize in Chapter 9.

2. **If you are working from a written text, read it *out loud* to yourself.** Use your ears, not just your eyes. These stories were meant to be *heard* and learned, as well as read and learned.

3. **Read it enough times to be able to recall the plot with a fair bit of accuracy.** The time this takes varies wildly. Some stories seem to float right into your mind. Some take a good long while. Don't worry, these variations are to be expected.

4. **Memorize the first thing you will say and the last thing you will say.** We feel that if you can get in and get out, then you can wander around the middle of the story for a very long time before anyone turns off the lights.

5. **Also learn the essential chants, songs, and phrases in the story.** It's not the story you memorize, just those few key names, repeated phrases, and musical bits that you *have* to say verbatim, just as written in your source material. It's not hard; they are meant to be easy to remember. There shouldn't be very many, and you'll know them when you see them. "Not by the hair on my chinny-chin-chin" has to be said just that way. Substituting "Not by my whiskers" just doesn't work. Learn these lines early and then reinforce this wording as you practice the story.

Now a few things *not* to worry about while learning a story:

1. ***Don't* worry about getting the words right.** We've said it before; we'll say it again. When you listen to a storyteller, you don't fret over whether he or she got the words right. You would never say to friends and family as you burst through

the front door with a juicy experience to share:" The greatest thing just happened to me! I can't wait to tell you about it. But first I'm going into my room, write it down, and be sure I get the words right."

2. ***Don't* fret over sequential order.** Yes, you want to get the scene-by-scene, event-by-event order right when you tell. But don't overly dwell on it while learning the story. And don't hold back from telling it until you're sure you have the sequence perfectly in mind. Think about personal stories you hear from friends. They jumble the sequence of events all the time, backfilling with flashbacks and forward jumps as new information pops into their heads. You have no trouble following each temporal and spatial jump through such stories. With telling and practice, the story will straighten itself out.

3. ***Don't* worry about gestures.** You take your body wherever you go, and so it will be a part of your storytelling. You do not design your gestures when making other presentations, so don't start now. Let gestures naturally evolve from your body and the story.

4. ***Don't* worry about how you sound.** The voice you have is the voice you have. You can certainly develop more expression or fiddle around with your volume, pitch, or rate. But the voice you have and use every day has been, and will be, plenty good enough to get your stories across.

You can go a long way on the suggestions above. That might just about do it. But maybe not. So we have added a list of additional approaches for those who find they need more. You need not use these. Indeed, some storytellers are very impatient with what they consider unnecessarily complicated approaches to a simple art form. If you are among them, avert your eyes.

1. **Divide the story into manageable scenes.** This is not difficult because stories tend to be episodic anyway. Some like to physically draw a line between scenes on a copy of their source material. Number and name the scenes and see if just saying each scene name helps you recall the places, images, and events of that scene.

2. **Develop additional sensory details.** Think of the Three Bears. You might be tempted to skip a detailed look at that kitchen. The scene will come alive for your *listeners* if you

see that kitchen *yourself*. What kind of bowls do the bears use? Thick, serviceable pottery? Do they sit at a table? Use napkins? Is it a fine day? Is the kitchen bright or dingy? Is the fridge covered with Baby Bear pictures held up by people magnets? Are last night's dishes still piled precariously in the sink?

3. **Create a storyboard and map the story on the board.** Rough, stick figure pictures are just fine for these drawings. For some learners, just seeing the story this way is a good memory boost.

4. **Get up and *move* that story.** Walk around while you tell, trying on some of the characters. Use your body to animate them and the tale. You don't have to use these postures and gestures when you tell. The idea here is to use your body to help fix the characters and story in your mind.

5. **Ask yourself some questions about the characters.** Do you know what makes them do what they do? What are they after in this story? Why is that goal important to them? Spend some time thinking about their places in the tale.

6. **Create an emotional memory.** As you learn each scene, ask yourself how each of the characters must be feeling. How would you be feeling? That emotional memory will stay with you and make it easier to recall the story and tell it with the appropriate feeling.

TOYS TO PLAY WITH

While touring Italy in the 1970s, Kendall met a door maker–door carver—a genuine Old World craftsman. He was rubbing a breathtakingly beautiful door relief with a polishing rag. Kendall asked if he was ready to hang the door. He said, no, it wasn't finished. Kendall asked him when it would be finished (it looked perfect to Kendall). He shrugged and replied: "When they take it away."

Like polishing that door, tellers can work on their telling skills forever, after the telling is long over. There is always a pause to adjust, a gesture to refine, a vocal inflection to improve. But these, as Gay, correctly calls them, are toys—stuff to spruce up the place.

Toys are *not* essential to your successful telling. Fold them into the way you learn and tell stories when you're ready. It's a lot like frosting a cake—not worth doing unless you have a well-made cake underneath. But once your cake-making skills are dependable, playing with the frosting provides a good deal of pleasure.

Don't worry about playing with your performance toys until you're comfortable with your telling and itching to find out what the storytelling tools at your disposal can do. Physical movement; vocal characterizations; physical characterizations; vocal tone, pace, pitch, etc.; gestures; and your physical relationship to the audience are among the toys you can develop both for your telling in general and for a particular story as you learn and practice the story.

But only when you're ready and it doesn't feel like work. When you're ready to add more variety and control into your telling, fine. Have at it! But don't think for a minute that you must consider these when you start your telling. Your natural storytelling system will serve you just fine until then. Remember: you are sufficient as you are.

CHAPTER 6

The Great Exception: Literary Tales

We take it back. There is one kind of story you have to memorize: the literary tale. Literary stories have an original, known author, not a reteller or an adaptor. The stories are housed under fiction, not folklore. It can be confusing, since authors sometimes re-create folktales, making a new story. Sometimes the same author may simply retell the story, making him or her not author, but adaptor.

Collections of literary stories to tell are well represented in the library, notably in the children's section. You will find Eleanor Farjeon there, keeping company with Richard Kennedy, Rudyard Kipling, and several others. Picture books, too, are literary stories to tell—and not just to young children. Chris Van Allsburg's work is a good example.

TELL IT OR READ IT

You could read it rather than tell it. Of course, all of the limitations of reading presented in Chapter 4 still apply. However, many of you are trained, practiced, and skilled in reading. It comes easily to you. You might want to read these stories and save your learning and practicing time for stories that will be faster and easier to learn.

But these are great stories, filled with wonder, magic, and the power to enthrall listeners—good reasons to consider telling literary tales.

TELLING LITERARY STORIES

Why do so many tellers put so much effort into memorizing? Because many of these stories are glorious and worth the trouble. The language is often evocative and compelling. They embody the same universality and timelessness found in traditional tales. Many of these stories are good yarns created by writers who are both story plotters and great wordsmiths.

Recitation of literary stories appeals to many librarians. The stories are well written, with evocative language that is catnip to any wordsmith. They've got a lot going for them. Some storytellers have devoted themselves to literary stories, and made an artistic reputation from their interpretations. You may do that as well, although it is more likely that you will find just a few literary tales that you think are worth the effort. We do not recommend that you start your storytelling career with literary tales. These are stories to work up to, as your telling becomes a comfortable second nature. It does take work to master them.

Good manners and good ethics dictate that you do your best to tell the story exactly as the author wrote it. Usually the language makes that a joyful task.

For example, Kipling's "Just So" stories have to be "just so." It will not do to say: "Go down by this really, really big river, deep too, with lots of trees, a lot of different kinds . . . ." Not when the author wrote: "The Kolokolo Bird said, with a mournful cry: 'Go to the banks of the great grey-green, greasy Limpopo River, all set about with fever-trees . . . '." If you choose to tell the story you have to tell it in Kipling's own words. The words are in large part what distinguishes it.

We know that literary stories were meant to be read, but can they be just as strong a tale when told? Perhaps so. Any number of literary collections began as stories told to family members for fun. These retain their oral antecedents and tell very well. But if you are unsure that the story is going to tell well, read it a few times to listeners and assess its potential.

Literary stories have lots in common with traditional tales. There are characters riding the plot, there are problems, villains, the full complement of robust life going on. There are differences, however, and not just in the language. Traditional stories have a minimum of descriptive passages, evocative language, subplots, characters, and incidents. Literary tales tend to have most of these in spades, especially descriptive passages. While they are lovely to listen to for awhile, recounting one more landscape scene dotted with geese and featuring a croquet match can be trying. Make the literary tale pass the traditional tale test. Is it a good, strong story, or just an impressionist romp?

We are loath to reinvent any wheel. We suggest you avail yourself first of the authors whose tales are often told. Start with Hans Christian Andersen, Richard Kennedy, or Carl Sandburg and use these worthies to measure new authors and their stories against. Story-length poems might also appeal to you. Every man we've ever known has gloried in "Casey at the Bat," "The Cremation of Sam McGee," or "The Rhyme of the Ancient Mariner." James Whitcomb Riley's "Little Orphant Annie" is similarly popular with those few women tellers who include poems in their repertoire.

Ballads are the musical equivalent of literary tales. Many lend themselves to being told and have all the qualities you seek in a tellable literary tale. Finally, don't overlook the collections of short stories, especially fantasy, and look at both Gary Paulsen and Ray Bradbury for excerpts as well as whole tales. Excerpts work too, so you may find yourself coming across a great passage to turn into a complete story. Tuck that one away for booktalking

LEARNING LITERARY TALES

Oh yeah, the memorizing part. Well, we all know it is hard work and time-consuming. We also know you can do it, because we have. We have done a lot of forgetting, too. To minimize the pain and maximize the investment, we offer a hint when memorizing literary stories.

When you learn a literary tale, you'll naturally focus on memorizing the author's words. But don't *just* memorize the words. Every story is more than the words—including literary tales. You are used to infusing your story reading with inflection, energy, rhythm, pace variation, and emotional interpretation of the characters and situations. You do the same thing when you naturally tell your own stories. In the previous chapters we've disussed doing that when you learn and tell a story.

However, memorizing a string of words is unnatural, and recalling that memorized stream requires focus and concentration. And that's the problem. Often so much concentration and focus goes into remembering the words that none is left over to give energy and meaning to the telling of those words. As is true for all stories, you have to expressf the story in large part by the *way you say it*.

As you learn the words of a literary tale, consider the mood and feeling of the story as well as the characters and their emotions, personality, intent, and struggles. Then the words can come alive for your listeners. It's like the difference between reading a Shakespeare play and watching the same lines brought to life and vivid meaning by trained Shakespearean actors. Your job with a literary tale is both to learn the lines and to fill them with energy, meaning, and life by the way you tell them.

It's work, but these stories are worth it.

CHAPTER 7

Playing with Practice

WHY PRACTICE?

By "practice" we mean telling the story out loud to live listeners before you tell it to your intended audience. Such practice telling of a story is not a requirement of successful storytelling; it's a tool. It's a valuable part of learning the story. After all, storytelling *is* telling. Many tellers (the two of us included) believe that telling a story is learning the story. Telling is the other half of learning—following after those activities presented in Chapter 5.

But did you ever practice telling personal incidents before sharing them with family or friends? No. Of course not—or *did* you?

Think back on your treasured family and personal stories. The first time you told the story of some new personal experience, it rarely came out as smoothly or as well-developed as during later tellings. The act of telling helped you edit and organize the story in your mind, create effective sequencing, cut out unnecessary digressions, and develop the relevant details you need to tell. Stories grow over time, and your telling of them gains flow, pacing, and energy as you tell them over and over again. That's practice. It's a natural part of your story development and refinement process.

Kendall often plays a game during workshops in which participants tell about a character or a past event three times, once to each of three different partners. He tells them that they will have one minute to tell their story each time. In truth, he gives them fifty seconds the first time, sixty seconds the second, and seventy-five seconds the third. Most participants can't fill their first fifty-second telling. Most participants also run out of *time* on the third telling.

Over three quick tellings, the story expands, develops, and takes on clearer interpretation and more vivid details. That's practice. Really, practice is nothing unnatural or onerous. You automatically do it all the time.

PLAY WITH PRACTICE

Approach practice not as mandated work, as drudgery, but as play time. Play with the story as you practice it. Treat practice like trying on dress-up clothes. Experiment with different wording, different characterizations, different voices. No need to keep it if you don't like it, but don't be afraid to try. Play with the process as you would while creating an outfit from individual pieces and accessories. You'll wind up with a better story and will be energized by the process of trying it on and making it fit with your style and flare.

You also want the greatest bang for your story practice buck. Here are ideas to make your story practice more effective and efficient:

1. **Before you tell it, tell *about* it.** Describe what happens and to whom. See how far you get. Don't worry about the actual wording or sequencing; just tell *about* it. Tell about the major characters as if you were describing a well-known friend. Feel free to include aspects of that character that you know don't actually appear in the text of the story. No, this doesn't mean that you'll include this level of character detail (some would call it *fluff*) when you tell. But the better you can see the characters in your mind, the more completely they will

appear in your listeners' minds when you present the words and details that *are* in the text of your story.

2. **Try telling it *right now*.** Yes, that's what we mean: right now. Since we tend to set great store on doing things until they are done, we, also, need to tell stories *before* they're ready to tell. And by the way, when is it ready to tell, anyway?

3. **You don't have to practice it *all*.** Just work on small pieces of the story when you have a free moment but not enough time to run through the entire story. This will let you focus more attention on the fuzzy parts.

4. **Mirror, mirror on the wall.** Cover the mirror. *Never* practice a story in front of a mirror. Never.

5. **Kinesthetic learning.** Gesture and movement can be effective learning techniques. Many of us are kinesthetic learners: we learn best right through the skin, like kids. Try telling your story (privately) by moving around a lot, gesturing, dancing, and walking. Some people find this freeing and learn about the story that way.

6. **Take a more detailed look around the story.** We introduced this idea in Chapter 5 with the Three Bears' kitchen. It won't hurt to use this technique again in between your practice tellings.

7. **Art as practice.** Some tellers find it valuable to sketch a series of quick stick-figure drawings that tell their story. As does any other practice telling, this storyboard game helps cement the story in your mind. As a bonus, drawing each scene encourages you to fully picture the space and place you'll tell about.

8. **Tell the story before a small audience.** This might mean the family (but only if they are really supportive), a few staff members, a friend or two, or your book club. We recommend that you *not* ask these groups for feedback or critique. They aren't skilled story and performance critics. They're your family and friends. Tell them the story, thank them for listening, and know that every time you tell it, you'll become more comfortable and confident with your telling of this story. These tellings are valuable practice, but don't treat them as more than that.

THE FINAL FOUR

If we were to distill all the advice and techniques in Chapters 5 and 7 into four bottom-line things to remember as you learn and practice telling a story, they would be these:

1. **The best way to *learn* stories is to *tell* stories.** This sounds counterintuitive, but it is one of the most reliable tenets of storytelling. No matter how much you prepare, how polished your presentation skills, you don't really create the story until you tell it to an intentional audience. Not off the cuff, not as practice, but as a planned, arranged telling. At the risk of sounding like we have spent too much time in California, we know that something happens when you tell; something surprising, something indefinable. Your well-prepared tale changes. The story dances across the bridge to your listeners and dances back to you. Your timing shifts, new words appear, the emphasis in a given scene subtly alters. You give one story and receive another one in return, changed but the same.

2. **It doesn't always feel right.** (And that's okay.) Most people are unaccustomed to telling stories in a formalized, intentional way. We know this because when we confess that, yes, we do tell stories for a living, we're likely to hear: "That's dying out, isn't it? It's too bad, huh?" But when Gay first began to tell, she remembers thinking, "This feels a little odd. Nice, but odd." When she told a story it felt contrived and awkward at first, something like trying to learn the tango. So it may be for you, but don't stop. Soldier on, for soon enough it will lose that "what am I doing here?" quality and you will ease into the confident, comfortable storyteller you were meant to be.

3. **Seeing is . . . seeing.** Nothing can convince fledgling tellers that storytelling works except doing it. No amount of witnessing and testifying to the power of storytelling is worth a fig. You have to do it to believe it.

4. **Less is truly more.** Remind yourself that this is a simple art form; it is not improved by making it more complicated.

CHAPTER 8

Glorious Tellings

You've chosen; you've learned; you've practiced. Only one thing left to do: tell.

The most important advice anyone can give you now is to do what feels comfortable for you and appropriate for your audience, your library, and its available space. That having been said, here are some tips that represent the collective wisdom and experience of many tellers to help you decide what will work best for you.

We speak here from personal experience. Both of us have made almost every mistake referenced in this chapter and know how easy it is to ignore these seemingly trivial concerns as you focus on your role as storyteller. Don't be penny wise and pound foolish. You have poured your time and energy into preparing yourself to tell. A minor oversight in your planning for the space and audience could derail your efforts.

BEFORE IT'S TIME TO TELL

While you and your story are what's important, neither exists in an aesthetic vacuum. You will tell stories in a particular place, at a particular time, to a particular audience. Librarians are good at advance planning, and that's going to come in handy here. Look at the elements you have to work with and treat yourself as a visiting artist, worthy of the best preparations you can provide.

Space

Your job as a storyteller and an event manager is to create a space for stories that is comfortable and protected. Evaluate the space that you have available, using the eyes of a guest performer. Is there a way to use the available space to protect and advance your purpose? You'll want to use the space to minimize disruptions and to suggest the nature of the occasion.

Children's programs are usually held in the open part of the children's area, or in a space set aside for programming or meetings. Other sorts of programs also use either the library proper or a meeting room. If the former is what you have, then the options for changing the space are limited. The options for adapting it are not. Try a fabric or screen backdrop (but not too busy) that is only used for storytelling. Perhaps you can arrange the seating so that listeners have their backs to the center of the room. If it is a sterile meeting room that holds the memory of city council meetings, is there a way to personalize it? Try using a backdrop here too, and place the chairs at an unexpected angle. Are there rugs or carpet squares to set out?

Easier by far to line folks up in rows, or a gentle arc. Chairs are unnecessary for little ones, but after fourth grade or so give young people the dignity of a formal seat. During family shows it is customary to seat small children down in front and adults in chairs behind. Resist this at all costs. It's much better to have families sit together so that parents can witness firsthand their children's delight with stories and share in that delight during the story. Stagger chairs so small ones can see.

Now look at the space as a storyteller and check light and sound. Can you be clearly heard without having to shout? Can you drop your voice to a whisper and still be heard at all? Where does the light come from? Will the audience be able to see you?

Finally, view the space as an audience member. Walk out into the seating area and sit down. Do you like it as a listener? Are you comfortable? Are there visual distractions that should be removed? As we said, this sounds like a lot of extra work. But this is work that can pay dividends during your telling.

Don't Go It Alone

You can't do it all. No teller can. Designate another staff member, a visiting teacher, or some other responsible adult to be "house manager." During your stories, you tell, and let that person manage the audience. If administrative questions arise—"Where's the bathroom?" "Is that story in a book I can check out?"—if disruptions or behavior problems surface, let the house manager handle it. Discuss it ahead of time so that person will know when he or she should or shouldn't step in.

Stage Arrangements

What will you want with you and near you when you tell? You may need to provide a chair, table, stool, or all of these. Be sure water is nearby. Some folks place a vase of flowers "on stage." That's fine, but any object must contribute to the event, not distract from it.

Setting the Scene

Storytellers traffic in enchantment. The stories will take care of most of that, but you can help it along. What is the signal that the stories will begin? Is there a special seat? Does a song signal the beginning? A chant? A poem? An object can do yeoman's work for you: a bell or drum as a summons; if you play an instrument, by all means do so, unless it means hauling the tuba into work. You might like to don an evocative garment that acts as a signal (but, again, not too busy). Mister Rogers endured many jibes for his sweater routine, but it was just that, a routine that separated work time from enchantment and make believe. It worked for him, and, with a little thought, it can work for you. Go ahead, create a sense of occasion.

Guide listeners into your seating plan as they arrive. Don't let them flop against the nearest convenient wall. Does this sound bossy? Remember, you've spent considerable time and thought to create the arrangement that will be best for listener and teller alike. So use it.

Before You Begin

Give yourself a moment to review the stories. Don't rehearse; just review quickly and simply, taking care to speak the first line of the story so you can get in, and the last line of the story so you can get out. Review any of those key lines and memorized bits that will appear in today's stories.

Choose your position. Are you going to stand or sit? Will you stay in one place, or have you grown used to moving around a bit?

Your listeners' ages help make the decision. An adult who stands in front of little kids can loom as large as a Macy's Thanksgiving Day float. Older children and adults are unsurprised by your standing, but even they will be uneasy if you stand in a small space, your toes inches from their own. Conversely, if older children are in chairs, will the back row be able to clearly see you if you sit to tell? During practice, have you made gestures or movements that would be awkward to do while sitting?

LET'S START THE STORY

Backstage usually doesn't exist in libraries. Oh sure, you can lurk behind the circulation desk, but mostly it is public space. That makes it particularly important to walk into the space you've created for your telling ready to tell. Many beginning tellers creep apologetically—as if being forced—into the performance space, resignedly square their shoulders, breath as if they are on life support and . . . begin. But, oops, you have already begun, and the audience has been unwillingly observers to your adjustments and tics. Prepare to tell before you tell.

Introduction

The occasion determines the introduction. You may be adding a story to an existing program, presenting a program of stories, or using a story as a counterpoint to a presentation. There are all manner of variations. In all cases *do* begin with something. If you are presenting one story only, or a program of stories, then an introduction gives you a moment to settle in and allows the audience to get a look at you, what you're wearing, and how you sound. That way, when you do begin your listeners are ready to really listen. Discipline yourself to keep it short, since a long introduction usually signals the teller's anxiety at beginning the tale.

Opinions differ about announcing the title of the story. Even we differ. One of us likes to announce the title and hence plug the book; the other likes to talk a little bit about the story (very briefly), giving the audience a small taste or a bit of information about the origin of the tale, and then state the story's title after the story is over. After this brief introduction, pause for just a moment to create a small space between your introduction and the beginning of the story.

Keep Moving

Now comes the good part: the story. Imagine that you and the story are standing there together. Step up together, and then you step back and let the story shine. Don't worry about an occasional lapse. This is not a high wire act, and you won't fall to your death if you miss something or other. The audience won't turn on you like a pack of wolves. Slow down and pause a moment if you need to. It will come back. Yes, it will. The audience will neither mind nor remember the lapse.

Slow Down

Keep the story moving, but don't be in a rush. Slow down. Let your listeners enter each scene and event. You have all the time in the world. Take it easy. Pause and take a breath. Pauses are amazingly effective and aren't used as often as might be. They build anticipation and suspense and give listeners a moment to sink deeper into the story. They are your little friends, too, since they allow your mind to stay ahead of your mouth and keep you and your story dancing to the same tune.

Your Partners

Storytelling is an equal opportunity art form. You get to tell, and the audience gets to help you. In fact, the only thing you should be aware of while you tell-other than the story-is the audience. You can chart your course and monitor your story's progress by watching the audience. Are they right there, with eyes on you, smiling at all the right places? Or are there subtle glances at their watches, shifting in their chairs? Let their re-actions guide you and you will alter your pace, your details, your telling as necessary. It's a wondrous gift to create the story through your audi-ence's guidance. Embrace it. There *is* one exception, though: very small listeners may be less able to control their bodies than you might wish. Don't be too sure that this is a lack of interest.

Grand Finale

Whether you've told just one story, or a full evening of tales, don't be in a hurry when it is over. Stay where you are when you are finished. Take a well-deserved bow, acknowledge the wild applause, and take your time before leaving. A race to the door is unseemly and unnerving, and it disrupts those moments when the story still lingers.

DON'T MUDDY THE WATER

Above all, do not apologize after you finish a story. Never. No mat-ter what happened during the telling. It does not contribute to the listen-ers' experience to hear what you forgot or regret or want to add. If they enjoyed the story and your telling, your post-performance disclaimer will diminish, even negate that enjoyment. Sure, there is the impulse to make it right. Resist it.

Let the story be. You may be eager to take questions or make com-ments about the story or stories after you are finished. It's a little like watching those outtakes or director's cuts on a DVD, and that can be fun and instructive. But if you do it after you've finished a story you become the observer/critic not the storyteller, and that diminishes the experi-ence. Let your listeners sit with the story. They don't need a full précis of the experience. To seize this opportunity to comment about the story's meaning, lessons, or importance to you is tantamount to announcing that the listeners' own experience is shallow at best and must be augmented by your own. Another to resist!

CELEBRATE

After your storytelling is over and the audience is gone, reserve a moment for private celebration. Celebrate what you and the audience have accomplished. Celebrate the success of your shared experience.

There will always be time to review your experience later and give it your full and critical attention. Not now. You too need time to absorb the experience and to claim it. You've done a good job. Enjoy!

KEEPING TRACK

The last thing to do is also the first: good record keeping. Keep track of your stories and your storytelling. You will want to develop your own method for filing and retrieving stories. The usual decisions and approaches to information management apply, and no one is better than library staff at making them. We have two different methods, but both of us have a hard copy of each story we tell, as well as a database of the stories on our computers. You may decide to organize the traditional tales by title, culture, theme, or all three. You want the system to serve you well, and to allow you to grab the right story quickly when an unexpected occasion for telling arises.

Many storytellers keep abbreviated forms of their stories for convenience as well—just a brief story outline with a beginning and ending sentence. This way you can tuck the ones you've chosen right into your requisite library tote and hit the road—school visit, community group, etc. You're set for a fast review before you begin to tell.

After the telling, it is time to reflect on the event. Both of us have a planning sheet for each appearance, and we use it to make notes about the audience's response, the suitability of the stories we chose, and how well the telling went. You will do more of this in the beginning. As time goes on, your experience as a storyteller will make it a less elaborate exercise. The planning sheet is still useful even then, because it reminds you of what stories you've told to what group. It's not a good day when you think your choices are new to your listeners only to have one comment, "I remember that story." Now don't misunderstand us, telling the same story to the same folks is no gaffe; we all like and need to hear tales again. You want to KNOW you're doing it, that's all.

If you are most interested in traditional, literary, or historical tales, you will read many before you find one you know you will want to tell. "I've got to remember that one for the future," you'll say. Yes, you do. But you won't. A cardinal rule is to make a copy of any story that attracts you, even if it's a mild flirtation. You know how we learned to do this, and it's a sad, bitter tale. We're still looking for that one. Have you seen it?

CHAPTER 9

First Aid

While learning to ride a bicycle, every child earns a Band-Aid™ or two, gathers a few scrapes, and merits a bit of minor triage—the stuff of good stories, or at the least, badges of honor. Storytellers can similarly benefit from learning a few basic first aid techniques to gently and safely handle the bumps and scrapes they may encounter along the way.

Don't worry about fixing performance mishaps as you start your storytelling career. Tell some stories. See what works well for you and what feels comfortable. If a particular telling feels more like a train wreck than an accomplishment, move on and tell others. It's all part of gaining your chops, as they say in the music business.

When the period of picking yourself up and dusting yourself off has provided more than enough experience in scrubbing out, it will be worth your while to pick up a few tools and techniques to head off those looming disasters that shine like a pair of high-voltage headlights, threatening to freeze you in your tracks and strip your mental gears.

TO MEMORIZE, OR NOT TO MEMORIZE? THAT IS THE QUESTION

We said it earlier. Don't memorize stories. But be honest. If you had to tell "The Three Little Pigs" tomorrow and held a copy of the story in your hands tonight, wouldn't you want to read the story over and over, trying to memorize the words and plotting sequence?

Memorizing is a deadly trap. It undercuts your storytelling in six important ways that almost guarantee you will not successfully, effectively tell the story:

1. **Memorizing is difficult and time-consuming**. Try it. See how long it takes you to memorize the words on this page. One page is a small part of a complete story. Memorizing is a frightfully slow and labor-intensive process.

2. **The words of a memorized story don't last.** Once you have memorized this one page, see how well you remember it tomorrow. Can you still recite it in two days? In four? We doubt it. Then you'll have to start all over again.

3. **Memorizing a story makes it difficult to tell the story with enough energy, enthusiasm, and expression**—key elements of your natural and successful storytelling. If your energy is diverted into recalling a string of words, not enough is left over to put into the telling of those words.

4. **The specific words a teller says are not the most important source of information for listeners**. Research shows that listeners internalize and remember the *gist* of a story, not your specific words. You don't help or improve the listeners' experience of the story by memorizing words.

5. **Memorizing a string of words makes it more difficult for you to use your natural storytelling style**. Your natural story-learning system is based on sensory images and feelings, not words. Memorizing words competes with the natural system you have developed and perfected over a lifetime of telling experience.

6. **You will rarely convince yourself that you have successfully memorized a story**—at least, not until you have told it a number of times, something you may never do. These doubts increase the probability that you *will* forget.

Don't memorize a story. Memorizing is the rocky road straight to performance disasters. If you are going to tell it, relax and tell it.

THE GREAT-AMAZING-NEVER-FAIL SAFETY NET

What should you *do* if you forget part of the story while you're telling? Even the Great Garibaldi Brothers, defying gravity as they soared high through the air of the Parisian big top in the late 1800s, had a safety net underneath them. Storytellers deserve no less.

We can almost guarantee that, at regular intervals, you'll forget while you tell. So what? No one will really care—besides you. The following elements of the Great-Amazing-Never-Fail Safety Net are designed to help you gracefully recover from your story slips.

Go Ahead and Forget

Yes, we mean it. No big deal. People do it all the time while telling stories. No teller seems to mind a momentary lapse when telling in an informal setting. You forget for a moment, pause, gather the story, and go on. Friends and family hardly notice and certainly aren't critical. Sometimes you even say, "Let me think here for a second," as you pause and mentally review the story.

Treat your role as a community storyteller in the same way. Launch into your stories with confidence and enthusiasm. If you happen to forget for a moment, shrug, pause to regroup, and continue as the story reforms in your mind.

Learn the Smile

A reliable secret to successful recovery from performance mistakes is—simply—to not act as if you made a mistake. How do you do that? Learn the smile, the oops-I-goofed-but-I'm-not-going-to-let-you- see-it smile.

Imagine the moment when you realize you've just made a mistake during your telling—forgotten to tell a piece of the story, missed one of those repeated phrases or rhymes, or simply forgotten what comes next. Yes, it will happen during your tellings. It happens to everyone. Don't despair. Stop, pause, and buy time while you mentally regroup without *looking* like you made a mistake and are trying to regroup.

Use the smile. What does it look like? Simple. First pause—stop talking. Second, smile and nod as if this were your favorite part of the story. Third, breathe, deep and slow. Take your time and remember that you are the only one who really knows what's coming next.

You're also the only one who has any notion that what comes next has momentarily danced off your mental desk top. So relax and smile.

It's easy to buy five or more seconds. That's a good long time for you to quiet your mind and let the story flow back in. Trust us, it will. You can, of course, extend the pause by repeating the last sentence you said and repeating the pause—smile, nod, breathe, and exhale.

Tell *About* the Story

We mentioned this as a story learning-technique. You can also use it when you tell.

The first few times you tell a story, you won't have convinced yourself yet that you *really* know the story. Some parts of the story remain annoyingly elusive. Knowing that these fuzzy sections are waiting to trip you up sometimes conspires to make you forget the parts you *do* know.

Eliminate the stress. Don't promise to tell the story, promise only that you'll tell *about* the story. Literally. Tell your audience that you want to tell them about a new story. We have each said, and heard other tellers say, "I want to tell you about a new story I'm working on." You have subtly changed the rules and the listeners' expectations.

Now launch into *telling* the story with all the enthusiasm you can muster—right up to the first section you are unsure of and reluctant to tell. Keep going if you can. There's no mandate to stop.

But if you feel at that moment that you must, then pause, smile, and say, "Isn't that a wonderful beginning?" Then tell *about* this part you are afraid you won't remember and won't tell well. Provide only a summary plot bridge to keep your audience from getting lost. As soon as you're past that part and are back to firmer story ground, pause, smile, and say, "Here is what happens next," and launch back into storytelling again. You'll switch back and forth between *telling* and *telling about* right up to your big finish, telling only those parts of the story you are comfortable and confident telling with energy and enthusiasm.

By not forcing yourself to muddle through the problematic sections, you never pull your energy and confidence out of the telling. When you tell, you tell with conviction. Listeners will be swept into the story, getting the best of your storytelling.

When You Remember You Forgot

You're fully engaged in telling, when, with a jolt of terror, you realize that you've left out a whole section of the story. Relax. Every teller does that.

Consider the informal stories you tell and hear. People forget parts all the time and, when they realize it, they merely stuff it back in wherever they are. We're used to hearing jumbled, nonsequential storytellings. With guidance, your listeners are fully capable of reordering the story sequence in their heads without getting lost.

The key to smoothly and successfully handling these moments is to neither look nor act as if you have done anything wrong (and that's right; you haven't). Don't cringe, grimace, or mutter dire curses at yourself. That will worry your audience and they'll leave the story to take care of you.

First, use the smile. Pause, smile, breathe and nod, as if you were taking a moment to relish this part of the story. Then choose one of the following: "There's something I haven't told you yet . . . " (not as a confession, but with intent) and tell them the part you earlier forgot. Perfectly true. You haven't told them yet (because you forgot). Or say, "There's something you need to know before we go on . . . ." Again true. (They need to know it *now* because you left it out *earlier*.) Or say, "Now, what *we* know but the wizard doesn't is . . . ."

What would this look like? Here's an example. While telling the "Three Billy Goats Gruff," you announce that, trip-trap, trip-trap, the first Billy Goat marches onto the fateful bridge—only to realize that you completely forgot to mention the troll.

No biggie. Pause, smile, breathe, and say, "Of course, we can peer under that bridge, as the Billy Goat cannot. And underneath . . . ." There you are, smoothly transitioned into the omitted part. Then repeat "trip-trap, trip trap" and return to the Billy Goat starting his trip across the span.

No one but you will suspect that the story didn't come out the way you intended, and your confidence will take a great leap forward. Even if some folks sense you've just completed an adroit save, they will admire the save and forgive the lapse.

What Comes Next . . . ?

Probably the greatest public speaking fear is to suddenly realize you have no idea what to say next. Your mind goes blank. Your mouth opens, and nothing is there to come out.

No problem. No damage has yet been done because no one but you knows you don't remember what comes next, and you have plenty of time to recover.

Again: Relax. Pause, smile, breathe deep and slow, and nod as if this were your favorite part of the story. Even chuckle softly to yourself.

There's a good ten seconds you can buy without having to say a word. Ten seconds is plenty of time for the story to return. If you remember, simply proceed with the story. They'll never notice a thing.

If the story hasn't reappeared in your mind yet, you need to verbally tread water and hold your spot in the story. How?

- **Repeat the last line.** Repeat it and again pause, nod, smile, and breathe. Repeat the line a third time as if it were a prophetic turning point of the story. Many tellers use this technique to add emphasis and power to specific words and moments. Blamm! There's another fifteen seconds to reconstruct the story and where you are in it. It will come back. Yes, it will.

- **Describe the scene you are in.** We rarely need more than a salient few sensory details we tellers have created and stored in our minds. Try wandering through these scenic details while your brain tries to figure out what happens next. It's easy to buy another fifteen to twenty seconds with this description. You have now bought almost a minute—a lifetime when you're on stage and plenty of time for you to conduct a systematic, orderly reconstruction of the story.

- **Ask them: "What do YOU think will happen next?"** This is only used as a safety net. Listeners should not be required to pony up some opinion or answer as a bride price for hearing the story unless this is a planned participation story. Even if it's an unfamiliar story, they'll likely be able to forecast the next part well enough to help you remember. If you need it, it's nice to know that the audience is there and capable.

- **Be brutally honest.** Tell them that you can't remember the rest of the story. They may not believe you and may yell for you to finish it *now*. Still, you're being honest, and it's valuable for them to see that their favorite storyteller is fallible and that a storyteller can forget and still survive. The key to making this work is to confess you've lost your way in a manner that suggests that the sun will still rise on the morrow and you will live to tell again.

The real points of the safety net are these: First, these are real, practical interventions that save most tellers most of the time. Second, as soon as you *believe* that you can extract yourself from a troublesome spot, you will. The trouble isn't forgetting. We all do that. The trouble is the mind-freezing fear of forgetting. Third, the only real mistake you can make while telling a story is to act like you have made a mistake. Until you act that way, you haven't. Last, and maybe most important, in reclaiming a story that has come unmoored: never, ever apologize and never, ever let your listeners see your anger or disappointment with yourself. If you indulge in either of those alarming responses, you take all of the energy in the room and place it where it doesn't belong—on you and your struggle. The story, not you, should always hold center stage.

CHAPTER 10

Owner's Manual

When you buy a new car, you want to go for a drive. You don't want to sit in the showroom studying the owner's manual. You want to know what the car can do. But eventually, you'll want to thumb through that manual to see what those mysterious buttons, knobs, and dials are for.

Same with storytelling. First tell some stories. Take your storytelling around the block a time or two. Kick the tires. Peek under the hood, but once you're well acquainted you may want to see what your storytelling machine can do, how it can develop. What are the elements of your storytelling machine that you might want to explore? Simple: you use your body, hands, face, and, of course, your voice.

First, a reality check. You employ these "toys" of yours each time you open your mouth, and you do so naturally, without affectation. Too much scrutiny can damage that ease and spontaneous style. We like to say it's like trying to find the soul of a frog. It is a fruitless exercise, and it kills the frog. So take the following suggestions and exercises with a grain of salt and deal with them only if you are getting restless and want to take on some refinements, or if you are dissatisfied with some aspect of your telling. Should you be inclined toward endless perfecting—that uncomfortable state that makes us alter who we are—then give the rest of this chapter a big skip until you find it helpful, not prescriptive.

You can find any number of books that explore the use, development, and control of each of these storytelling "toys." Most of them can be found under storytelling, but not always. The confusion about what storytelling really IS extends to where one can find materials. Manuals and advice about body and voice can also be found under theater, acting, improvisation, and dance. Should you be particularly interested in one toy or another, you will have lots of resources to use. Here we offer only a brief survey, with a few quick activities to give you enough to go on in the meantime. In short, let's play around.

AN OPENING GAME

How you say a story (the vocal tone, volume, pitch and speed you use combined with gestures, facial expressions, and physical movement) is important. Listeners gain lots of information from how you say it. In fact, **HOW** is a full and co-equal partner of **WHAT**.

Community storytellers can consider this good news. You already know *how* to tell an effective story. Remember, you do it every time you present a book or entertain your family. You've been developing, testing, and rehearsing that skill all your life. You use and hone that skill every day in the library.

Don't believe that you are already highly skilled in the arts of *how* to tell a story? Here's a quick game to prove to yourself just how good you are. Consider either of the following sentences/questions:

YOU WANT ME TO GO THERE.?

I'LL HAVE HER DOG DESTROYED.?

The interesting thing about these is that you can place the emphasis on any of the words in either sentence and have it make sense. You can say them as either statements or as questions and make them make sense.

Try it. Say one out loud to another person, placing the emphasis on the first word, say it as a statement, and make it sound real and natural. Then change the emphasis to the second word, and so forth.

Awkward, isn't it? Yet you do this expertly every time you open your mouth to talk. In fact, you always do more than this. You also have an attitude, or emotion, you effectively communicate along with sentence emphasis.

Try it. Say the sentence again, and along with placing the emphasis on the chosen word, adopt one of these five emotional attitudes to express: sarcasm, joy, confusion, fear, or relief.

Difficult, isn't it? Yet you do this flawlessly every time you speak. In fact, you do more than this because you also incorporate physical movement and gestures into your speech.

That skill you naturally possess is more than sufficient to meet the mandates of your storytelling. When you learn the sights, events, and emotions of a story, your natural oral skill will take over and express the story as effectively as it does your normal daily communications.

VOICE

Your voice carries the story. Unless you use sign language exclusively, or mime, you cannot tell a story without your voice.

Most if us remember the first time or two that we heard our voices on tape. Memorable, wasn't it? But WHO was it? What happened to that mellifluous, dulcet tone? Who put in the nasal whine, that reedy little wheeze? We hear our voices through the bones in our faces and heads, not just through our ears. The taped voice is a startling revelation.

Tough truth: your voice is your voice. It may not be the one you would have chosen in The Catalogue of Beautiful Voices, but it is the one you have. It takes a great deal of money and a good voice specialist to change that with which you were born. Don't waste your money, unless there is a diagnosable problem. In storytelling, the conviction and engagement with which you tell are important, not the trained quality of your voice. Some would say that voices betraying theatrical training are an impediment. It is said that President Lincoln was a consistently effective speaker even though his voice was regularly described as thin, high-pitched, and whiny.

Having said that, it is still useful to explore the vocal toys you can use when you tell. Remember: the trick is to avoid any vocal techniques that make you feel self-conscious. All of us use these instinctively because the voice is a supple, responsive instrument. Taking a moment to review them will allow you to fool around. It might be fun.

Here they are: rate, volume, and pitch. Each can be used to develop a character or to insert color and interest into your voice as you tell the tale.

Rate

We use rate each time we speak. Rate is how rapidly or slowly you speak. The relative speed of your delivery can suggest gender, emotional state, age, and more.

Here's an example you can try. Repeat this line adapted from Alfred Noyes's romantic old poem "The Highwayman": "The highwayman came riding, riding, riding, up to the old inn door." Just say it in a conversational tone, not slow, not fast. Now we're going to treat it as a piece of choral music and score it. The italicized words are to be said with speed, the regular text more slowly.

Here we go: "The highwayman came riding, riding, riding, *up to the old inn door.*"

Now try it in reverse: "*The highwayman came riding, riding, riding,* up to the old inn door."

Which one marries text to the rate? The second one, we think, but either way, the rate influences the words. You can also choose just one word to build up to and slow down from. In this example, it would be "UP". Try that.

Rate suggests age. We know that young children tend to speak more rapidly when there is something on their minds. Preschoolers' words tumble over each other in a contest to get out first. When adults speak rapidly, it suggest several possible states: panic, alarm, argument, or excitement. Conversely, very slow, deliberate speech can be intimidating, suggesting menace or danger. It can also imply relaxation, deliberation, or ambivalence, among other things. You can give a very subtle reading of a character in your story just by using rate.

Pitch

Voices fall naturally into a wide range of pitch, from high to low. Very high voices are suggestive of young children (or a stereotypic voice for the elderly). Middle pitch implies a woman, and low pitches are often perceived as male. Hold on, though . . . women can have very low voices and the occasional man can have a natural falsetto. You can play around against type to develop unusual characterizations, but the basic assumptions about pitch will usually serve you the best.

Take our famous ursine family of plain speakers, the Three Bears. Each bear has a distinct age and gender. Although you could develop a distinctive voice for each one, using your favorite cartoon characters, you might like to keep it simple by using high, middle, and low pitches for them. Pitch, like all vocal toys, suggests emotional state. The squeaky voice of nervousness, the low growl that says "watch out": these and many more can telegraph what a character is feeling. Even though your small bear has a high voice, within that are ranges of high to low that can provide emotional coloration.

Volume

Volume is a big toy. It muscles into the character and the story and slings its weight around. It's a grand and effective toy, but don't overuse it. Don't let it run the show. What do we mean? Use your conversational voice as your norm, with the volume rising and falling according to the meaning and emotion of the text to add texture and color. Volume extremes (shouts and bellows that cause listeners to wince and cover their ears, or whispers that make them strain to hear), like a favorite pungent spice, are best if used judiciously and sparingly.

Loud voices announce emotional state right away. "Don't you raise your voice to me!" we say with our own voices rising. Anger, fear, aggression—all of these come with increased volume. Big sounds can suggest distance as we shout into space. Low volume draws the listener closer, promotes intimacy, and sometimes suggests suspense.

Effective tellers use this toy throughout a telling, sometimes speaking very quietly and sometimes loudly, depending on what's happening. The bold contrast between a whispered, low voice and a sudden shout is the hallmark of the "jump" tale, like the old ghost story that begins "In a dark, dark . . . ". Try that story and watch with satisfaction when your listeners "jump" at your loud moment.

GESTURE AND MOVEMENT

Gesture and movement encompass a wide range of motion, from a simple hand movement up to a fully mimed tale. The former is informal, often unconscious, the latter planned and choreographed.

Here is the grim news: your body always comes with you when you tell. You can't leave it behind to wait patiently for you to finish. Even more than voice, our bodies cause us no end of trouble. We are never satisfied with the way we look. Too tall, too short, too thin, too wide, weak chins, beady eyes. It's never right. It stands to reason then that we would become self-conscious when we bring our imperfect bodies out for scrutiny as we tell.

Here's the good news: your body and face are not the important parts, the story is what counts. Your listeners look at you, past you, and through you as they become more absorbed in the story. Remind yourself of this before you play with the gesture toys. One step toward that end is to understand the limits of gesture and movement, that is, to understand what types of information can be effectively and easily communicated through gesture and movement and which cannot.

Most of the moving and gesturing you do is natural and unaffected. You raise a hand or shake a finger without really knowing it. That is as it should be. The absence of movement, sitting stock still, whether out of nervousness or fear, is disquieting to your listeners. Bodies move when communicating. It's just instinctive. So let yours off the leash and give it permission to cut up. This is easier with young children than with older kids or adults. Little ones are exuberant listeners and will move and sway right along with you. Try to acquire the same level of physical comfort with adults and older kids that you have with small children. It may take awhile.

One technique seems to help almost everyone. In private, tell the story without words. Use only your body to tell the story. Do it several times. The next time you tell the story you may well find that you are physically more free than you were before.

Movement and gesture are like just about anything else. They work as organic, natural outcomes, not as a planned attack. You cannot create a movement or gesture for a character as if it were a garment to shrug off later. When you first tell a story you may have very few gestures or movements. It is only after repeated tellings that these appear, often unbidden, to help define a character or moment in a story. Forcing a gesture or movement into the tale almost always appears contrived. That's because it is a contrivance. Paying attention is a more successful approach. As you notice how your gestures and movements evolve, you can incorporate them into future tellings.

Stories take place in a space. Gesture and movement allow you to explore the uses of that space. Walking to another part of the "stage," crouching or stooping, reaching high—all these and dozens more can energize your tale and telling.

There are a few pitfalls to watch out for:

- **The roamer:** Are you constantly on the move? Aimlessly drifting around as if you could find the story somewhere? Stop. Stand still, or sit. Place some part of your body against something, a table, for instance, and ground yourself.

- **The tennis match:** Do you walk to one side for one character and march a few steps away for the other guy? No need. Use one of the vocal toys to distinguish between them and let your audience recover from the whiplash.

- **The concealer:** Do your hands hold each other for comfort? Do they creep into your pockets to hide? Are they behind your back? Let them out. Give them a life. Hand gestures are a natural way to communicate.

- **The creeper:** Do you sidle apologetically into the storytelling space, talking all the while? Take physical command. Straighten those shoulders and walk purposefully into the space. You're on so let your body take over.

A final truth: the body never lies. Your voice may disguise your intentions, but your body will reveal them. We know this. We watch people fiddle with their clothing, or tap their fingers, unable to control their impatience. We see people back away from what alarms them. Your body will communicate what you are feeling, so it is prudent to pay attention.

If you are so self-conscious that it impedes your telling, it is time to take action. Try a mime or improvisation class; maybe an exercise class will do the trick. It doesn't matter what you choose, but giving your body an opportunity to work out and get crazy will be time and money well spent.

Here's a simple exercise that lets you experiment with the look and feel of gestures. Remember, it's just a game. Be extravagant with your gestures.

Create a simple, three- or four-sentence story. Then create a specific gesture for every word in that story. One word, one gesture. One gesture, one word. Some words—articles and prepositions, for example—do not lend themselves to clear gestures. But you still must create a gesture for each and every word in the story. "Gestures," of course, are not limited to hand movement and may include body movement and facial expression.

Practice saying the story a time or two while performing each of the gestures you have created. Now "tell" the story to an audience. Let them know you will use gestures *only*. You will not speak any words in this performances of the story. Just for fun.

This is not a game of charades, where a gesture is repeated until understood. Don't encourage the audience to blurt out what they do, or do not, understand. You'll tell the story at normal storytelling cadence, just as if you were actually telling the story with words. The audience watches in silence until the story is over.

What do gestures effectively communicate? Action verbs (like *jump*), most emotions, direction, position, size, and shape. However, gestures often are better at portraying phrases or concepts than individual words.

Also notice the energy and delight gestures carry. These stories are fun to watch even when you haven't a clue what the story is about. It wasn't the story that was so attractive; it was the gestures through which it was told. Gesture is a compelling toy.

CHAPTER 11

Storytelling Extras

A story that is well told, by an engaged storyteller, needs nothing more. Additions like props, participation, and such speak more to style than to necessity. We really do think that anyone can enjoy telling stories, even just at an informal level, but we do not think that *anyone* can effectively use each of these add-on performance toys. Talent isn't the deciding factor. Each of these add-ons requires some stage management, and it must fit with your natural style and inclinations. It's a question of attraction.

Consider the list below as your own personal list of accessories. Clothing allows us to define our style, how we like to look, and these small additions to stories present the same opportunities for fun, for extending the story. They also present opportunities for unsuitable choices that can eclipse the story and the storyteller. To that end we have suggested some benefits and some deficits of each "accessory" listed. The same questions and measures apply here that reign in the dressing room: Is this comfortable? Does it fit me? Does it upstage me and what I'm wearing? How much care will it take? Does the investment equal or exceed the utility? Beyond this list of tit-for-tat questions, there may be times when it comes down to, "Oh, I just *love* it. That's all." And that's fine too.

FLANNELBOARDS

The beloved, dark felt-covered board that holds the little felt figures is more likely to take a star turn in the preschool storytime where it is a reliable staple—most often used for children under six.

The Plusses

1. **An old story can become a new one by telling it with the addition of the board.** "The Little Red Hen" becomes a fresh tale when wheat pops up for all to see.

2. **Young listeners may be able to follow the narrative more easily with the visual cue of the felt pieces.** As the pieces come and go and the story progresses, the watcher-listener can track the plot. For those struggling with language and learning, the little figures and pieces can help a lot.

3. **It's a good way for listeners to connect words with images.** The porridge from Goldilocks is easy to define when the steaming pot is visible on the board.

4. **It provides a simple change of pace.** A program of flannelboard stories would be like a dinner of desserts: too visually rich and ultimately unappealing. Slipping just one into an otherwise conventional program adds the needed spice.

5. **It may be a step for those who are uneasy about "putting the book down."** At least that's what seems logical. We're not sure. Sometimes the best way to overcome the fear of solo storytelling is to just do it. We do admit, thought, that this might be a good transitional step. Try telling familiar stories with the flannelboard and then telling the same ones alone.

The Minuses

1. **Flannelboarding is unavoidably fussy.** There is the putting pieces up and taking them down, smoothing them onto the board, picking them up, putting them aside. It seems fidgety and busy.

2. **The pieces *always* fall off.** Well, almost always. That's just the way it is.

3. **Traffic management is difficult.** It is difficult to tell, arrange the pieces, watch the listeners, etc. The teller unintentionally tends to direct listeners' attention to the board more than one would like.

4. **Kids may watch the board, not you.** And that's particularly regrettable because you're the one in possession of the story.

5. **Felt figures and objects are, by definition, static.** Unlike puppets, they don't move, and they aren't three-dimensional like props. (This argues for simple, bold designs that are eye catching and colorful.)

PROPS

Props are objects used in the course of telling the story. This large class of objects includes folk toys, paper-folding, musical instruments, string tricks, artifacts, scarves, etc.

It's decision time. You're going to tell "Little Red Riding Hood." But should you carry a cloth-covered basket to dangle over your arm when you tell about Red? Should you take an ax and hold it when you tell about the woodsman? Why not take a painting of a cottage in a forest clearing?

Should you really drag this walking garage sale to the library just to tell this one story? Should you dutifully pull out each item at the appropriate times during the story? Won't they make the story seem more real?

The answer is a skeptical "possibly." Consider the plusses and minuses.

The Plusses

1. **The prop may be essential or integral to the story.** This is especially true if you are adapting a children's picture book. *Crictor*, Tomi Ungerer's delightful book, can be retold, but not without the Big Guy. Many storytellers have used the requisite six-foot snake puppet to good effect. Folding-paper

tales obviously require, well, paper-folding. The same is true of stories featuring a musical instrument. Hard to do a good job without them.

2. **The prop provides cultural exposure through appropriate objects.** We know two fine California storytellers, Pam Brown and Martha Shogren, who are adept at using objects that are culturally relevant to the stories they choose. We particularly enjoy Pam's use of origami and small puppets. Martha doesn't use props during the tales, but afterward brings out a beautiful object from the culture to show the listeners.

3. **The prop provides a visual clue or enhancement.** A prop may also be important, if not precisely necessary, if an unfamiliar object is used in the tale. This is most likely when the tale refers to a tool or activity like spinning. Showing the object can employ an efficient visual shorthand when the explanation might weigh down the narrative.

4. **Props can be simply magical.** It's true. Beautiful, unusual and evocative objects cast their own spell. We all like to see cool stuff. As long as it contributes to the story and doesn't upstage it, go ahead. Have some fun.

5. **A musical instrument can add another artistic dimension.** An instrument can provide background, sound effects, melody or accompaniment for a song that appears in the story.

6. **Props add some modest razzle-dazzle.** Nothing wrong with a little glitz on occasion. Make that on *rare* occasions.

7. **They're fun.** Sometimes, props are just fun. The right props woven into the right story can be an extra delight for your listeners. Just make sure the story can tolerate the disruption of the props and that the props you use will have the desired effect.

The Minuses

1. **Who's running this story anyway?** Using anything except your voice and body can be a juggling act. Will your manipulation of the stuff be a distraction that will distance you and the listeners from the telling? Are they worried that you'll drop one of the balls?

2. **Does the prop enhance or detract from the story?** Is this a better story with the prop? Do you really need it? Creating stories for use in paper-folding, paper-cutting, string tricks, and other simple crafts is a busy little industry. The problem is that the stories can take a back seat to the activity. A story created just to be a showcase for the skill or handicraft lacks the depth and timelessness of a traditional tale. Be sure the story you choose is sturdy enough to be worth telling, not just an afterthought.

3. **Props can be a distraction, and interfere with listeners.** This is an oral art form. Enough said. Alright, not quite enough. As you brandish a new prop, listeners are pulled out of the story's images to stare at this thing you hold. Where'd you get it? How'd you make it? Is that really what you want?

4. **Listeners do not need props very often.** The whole idea of storytelling is that listeners imagine the story inside their heads. The more props you pull out, the more you keep them from their appointed task.

5. **This stuff takes time.** The time you may spend in the local import store, or in sewing, polishing, repairing, and cutting, could be spent working on the story.

Make It Work for You

1. **Try telling the story without the prop.** Was anything missing? Yes? Okay, add it to the tale.

2. **Decide where the prop belongs.** If it is necessary to the audience's understanding of the story, then show it in the beginning, with a bit of introduction. Don't rush. Give listeners a chance to look it over. If it isn't essential to the tale, consider showing it after the story is finished.

3. **Rehearse using the prop** to minimize the price that the listeners pay for its inclusion.

4. **Leave it out, or put it away?** If you will use a prop periodically (like a musical instrument) leave it out. If it is one time only, well then . . . decide. But decide in advance. Do you want listeners to focus on the prop after you've used it? Will it be awkward or time-consuming to stuff it away? Will it get in

your way as you tell the rest of the story? Use the prop during a practice telling and see what will be best for you and your listeners.

5. **Don't oversell the prop.** It doesn't matter that you bartered for it on your fabulous trip to the Falklands, or that you spent twenty-five hours making it from crushed egg cartons. While you tell a story, the story must be the central focus.

6. **Less is more.** How many props is too many? Answer: only you know. We think that, as is true for so many other aspects of storytelling, less is definitely more.

COSTUMES

A costume is clothing that is in contrast to your regular garments. Costumes can be period pieces or a collection of garments and accessories that are eye catching and festive.

The Plusses

1. **Costumes reveal character and period.** The historical costume can do some of the telling for you. By looking at you, the audience sees the period and the class the clothing implies. When you dress as a commoner, no one will mistake you for the king, for instance.

2. **Costumes make for a fancy occasion.** Costumes are crowd pleasers. Those who tell stories outside often dress to attract an audience. Festive, eye-catching clothing can set a mood and theme for your presentation.

3. **Costumes set the stage for stories told in the first person.** The most obvious application is for historical stories, where the eyewitness teller recounts his or her experience. Places like Colonial Williamsburg have known this for decades. Fantasy has a place also, since the requisite princess can dress for success, too.

4. **Costumes teach.** Most folks under sixty have rarely, if ever, seen spats. Wearing a pair can educate as well as delight the audience.

The Minuses

1. **You're stuck.** Costumes are simply props you don't have the luxury of setting aside. You cannot change your character easily, and cannot change the period at all.

2. **Glad rags may mislead your audience.** If you dress in some get-up that features eye-catching, buffoonish fabrics and jewelry, you risk becoming "Carbuncle the Clown" or some other generic children's performer—but without the clown act or magic tricks.

3. **You can't switch gears.** You are tied to the period of the costume. The alluring princess dress you donned for the first story means you're stuck in the realm. The alternative is one we have both seen: the storyteller races to a hastily arranged sheet to perform a genteel version of "take it all off" to get to that next story. Not a pretty picture.

4. **It seemed like a good idea.** Library staff is prone to costuming during programs for holidays like Halloween. Depending upon the site, one will find everyone on the staff in full ghoulish garb. It can be fun. It can also be full of effort and uncomfortable.

5. **You'll focus on the costume**. If you wear a rare, historical, or valuable costume, you'll be worried about getting it dirty, mucked up with sticky fingerprints, or torn during a dramatic gesture. Your focus on protecting and presenting the costume pulls you away from your primary mission: telling the story.

Make It Work for You

1. **Take the most reasonable approach.** Don't fight the costume. Choose a story that matches the costume and vice versa: a first person story from the period.

2. **Don't actually wear it.** Character costumes are almost as dramatic and effective if you bring them in on a hanger. Then they become props.

3. **Create a "storytelling costume."** Use the strengths of costuming and develop your own garment or accessory that sig-

nals, "It's me! The Storyteller!" Many librarian- and teacher-tellers have a hat, a vest, a coat, an apron, or a shawl that they wear whenever they tell stories and only when they tell. It's quite useful if you are usually dressed in the "Librarian Uniform" that says you're all business. Use it to give a visual cue to your listeners: This is it; we're telling stories now.

PUPPETS

Puppets include finger puppets, hand puppets, marionettes, and dolls used as talking, moving, acting characters during a story.

The Plusses

1. **Puppets are REAL for young listeners.** They are more real than you are during the story. Children will interact with the puppet completely.

2. **Puppets can misbehave** extravagantly during a story without causing mayhem among listeners.

3. **You can have a conversation with your puppet.** This affords you an opportunity to talk to the puppet and thus have two participants telling the story. That's fun for little kids.

4. **Puppets can act as the court fool.** Our friend Willy Claflin, a brilliant puppeteer and very witty fellow, has as many followers among adults as he has among children. The antics of Maynard Moose, his puppet alter ego, make small ones giggle, and his comments on the body politic make adults laugh as well. The court fool could speak the truth to the king with wit and tomfoolery. A puppet can do the same, with you as straight man.

5. **You can reveal another side of yourself.** Mister Rogers was a famously shy man who could become someone else with a puppet companion. So can you.

6. **Puppets can be just a delight.** When used well and made into an integral part of storytelling, puppets can be a crowd-pleasing joy. Puppets cross simple storytelling with

scripted play making, but if that appeals, puppets can be an effective addition.

The Minuses

1. **Puppets always upstage the handler. Always.** Puppets are the ultimate prop. They always take the audience. Always. Extract a skuzzy, featureless finger puppet of indeterminate age, genus, and phylum, push it onto your finger, and that puppet instantly becomes real and important. The puppet IS the story.

2. **You lose one of your hands.** Your hand is no longer yours. It belongs to the puppet.

3. **Puppets are REAL for young listeners.** Although puppets are irresistible to many small children, conversely, some are at best puzzled, at worst genuinely frightened, of the bewitching little characters.

4. **Some dexterity is required.** Not much, but some. If you choose a simple hand puppet whose movements are limited, you can get away with not doing very much. Complex puppets require complex movements.

5. **You have to make puppets to fit your story.** Not just any puppet will do for a story. The puppet has to match the character it represents. That means that you'll have to either custom make (or buy) your puppets, or revise the story so that puppet and story match.

6. **Puppets mandate extra practice.** Puppets introduce two new aspects of your story that need practice: your general puppet skills and the choreography for what your puppet is going to do while you tell the story. This means lots of extra practice with this upstart attention grabber after you have learned the story. The puppet is depending on you to make it move and act as it should—every moment, start to finish of the story. But those who have watched good puppet shows know the effort can be well worth it.

Make It Work for You

1. **Above all, keep it simple.** Let the puppet do the work and you take a bemused back seat.

2. **Make it a good fit.** Consider puppets only if you like them enough to shoulder the extra work, if they fit with your natural storytelling style, and if they fit well with your story.

AUDIENCE PARTICIPATION

Audience participation uses the audience to contribute to the story. That inclusion may be either planned or improvised on your part. You may rehearse the audience on their part(s) or not. It may include vocal or physical responses or both. These responses can include chants, repeated phrases, songs, gestures, movements, and, sometimes, guesses and opinions.

Audience participation runs the gamut from the subtle to the outrageous. Some tellers place specific activities along this continuum according to the size and complexity of the audience's participation, some by the amount of managerial control effort the teller must expend. We have broken our discussion of audience participation in half, using as the dividing line whether you physically bring audience members up on stage with you (a "Cast of Thousands" story), or do not. This first part covers audience participation when you keep them out in the audience.

The Plusses

1. **Participation works.** It is built into scores of stories. That's because it works. It works to assist listeners in remembering the story through chants, songs, rhymes, and movements. Just as we all make up mnemonics to remember a parking place, a grocery list, Henry VIII's wives, so participation helps listeners keep the story.

2. **Participation is an unrivaled way to engage young children.** As all storytellers know, when you ask a child to "help" with a story, you don't have to ask twice. Kids are ready. With participation, the storyteller gathers the energy and high spirits of young listeners and directs it toward telling the story together.

3. **It is an equal opportunity device.** Participation does not require anything extra. Anyone can do it.

4. **It's a good change of pace.** One participation story can vary the offerings, giving a nice change of pace in a longer program.

5. **It's fun.**

6. **Many people are kinesthetic learners.** Vocal and physical roles help them retain the story.

The Minuses

1. **It's easy to overuse this technique.** One or two participation stories give a pleasing texture to a program, but more amp up the audience and feed the cultural assumption that children, in particular, always, always need those colored lights.

2. **Assigned, rehearsed participation can pull listeners out of the story.** The excitement of being a contributing "cast member" can upstage story content. Kendall conducted a study that showed that children tend to remember their participation and *not the story*. (See "Note" at the end of the chapter for a description of the study.)

3. **Traffic management is a necessary component.** A roomful of children can quickly get out of control when asked to participate. This technique requires some forethought. How will you signal the beginning of the participation? How will you ensure that it will end?

4. **You can oversell the idea.** Your instructions for how and when to participate should be brief, simple, and fast. There is no need to rehearse, to review crowd control, and to conduct. Simply repeat what you wish listeners' to do, and then move on. Children, especially, are very good contextual learners and will catch on. If you teach the movement or vocals until everyone is well rehearsed and compliant, your performance will be over and the kids will be at recess. Relax.

5. **Participation engages the listener, but nothing replaces a quiet, compelling story from the storyteller alone.**

Make It Work for You

1. **Different levels, different guidelines.** We think it's best to split the way you think of audience participation into three separate situations and approach each differently.

   • **Situation 1: Encourage seemingly spontaneous participation.** When audience members spontaneously, verbally interact with story situations or call out to story characters, they participate in the story without being pulled out of their story images. Even pre-teens will spontaneously chime in with repeated lines in a story—if the teller sets it up and encourages that participation.

   Set it up by *how* you say key repeated lines. Add fixed gestures and body movements to reinforce the pattern of those lines. Say the lines slowly and rhythmically while smiling and nodding at the audience. By the second or third appearance of these lines, the audience will jump in all on their own.

   You can also tell stories the audience knows and have a character stumble over well-known lines. Younger audiences will always spontaneously dive in to make sure the characters get it right.

   What does that look like? Consider the wolf's huffing, puffing, and blowing line. You know the one. Say it with a slow, rhythmic head nod and rolls of your hands to encourage participation. "I'll huff . . . and I'll Puff . . . and I'll . . ." (pause, pause). As you expectantly arch your brows, every child in the room will spontaneously join in to finish the line. Alternately, you could have your wolf forget or stumble over the line. "And I'll, uhh . . . blow your house up. . . In? . . . Over? . . . " Again, every child will leap to the rescue to verbally straighten out you, the momentarily befuddled wolf.

   You may also pause during the story and, as either a story character or the story narrator, ask some story-related question of the audience. It's best if the question is really rhetorical and your continuation of the story doesn't depend on their answer. This unrehearsed interaction as part of the story is delightful for younger audiences, and—as is true at classic melodrama theater—fun even for adults.

- **Situation 2: Assigned, prerehearsed participation.** At this level, you will assign roles to part or all of the audience, but roles that keep them in their seats. Assign and rehearse audience lines only when you want the experience of participation to be the focus. Make sure that the lines (or gestures) you force them to repeatedly say will be fun, memorable, and worth their while. Be sure the time and effort to teach them their lines and the extra work to manage and control their participation will be worth it. This activity is best for preschool and primary ages. But keep their lines and gestures short.

  While telling the Jewish folktale "It Could Always Be Worse," (see the excellent version by Harve Zemach and Margot Zemach), you could assign different sections of the audience to cluck, moo, or grunt to represent the various groups of animals that are, one by one, stuffed into the house. Questions to consider: How will you cue them to start? More important, how will you cue them to *stop*? Rehearse your control plan as much as you do their assigned lines.

- **Situation 3: Take the seat belts off.** Adding movements to the audience's assigned participation lets them rise up out of their seats (or up off the floor) and flop about the room like beached mackerel. It's chaotic fun for them, but a potential nightmare for you. It is easy to lose control of the audience, and difficult (at best) to regain it. Don't tread into these mine-filled waters unless you are sure your management plan will keep you in control. Our advice is to use this type of participation sparingly and only with young children.

2. **Make it easy.** You can encourage, even plan for, this kind of participation. You can repeat the desired phrase or movement slowly, smiling all the while, slowing down your delivery. By the second or third try the audience members jump right in all on their own.

3. **Watch for a good opportunity.** Sometimes during the story an opportunity for participation just jumps right out. The audience usually leads the way, and you can take advantage of it. This technique is tailor-made for spontaneity and improvisation.

"CAST OF THOUSANDS" STORIES

These are stories in which you bring audience members up on stage to help you tell the story. "Cast of Thousands" stories combine participation with theater. Audience members are recruited on the spot to take part in the story that is "performed" before the rest of the listeners. Not extensively rehearsed, this technique takes advantage of the moment and uses a well-prepared story with several characters and a simple plot line.

The Plusses

1. **This is chaotic fun.** A natural for family programs, this is wild. Kids and adults can be recruited willy-nilly and pressed into service. There is fun in the transformation and in the "on-stage" negotiations and arrangements. Best for a large crowd.

2. **This can showcase an old story and make it new**. With audience members transformed into pigs, elves, or the Bremen Town Musicians, the story becomes new.

3. **This creates opportunities for spontaneous story making.** The very act of hauling folks out of the audience signals that this isn't going to be rehearsed. Give folks permission to ad lib a bit and add to their characters. Part of the pleasure is seeing what the cast can come up with.

The Minuses

1. **It's a minefield.** So be fully prepared before attempting this one. It might not work or that it will be difficult to control. Some library storytellers are more comfortable with this notion than are others. Let your temperament be your guide.

2. **It's all about traffic management.** You are going to recruit, manage, and coax the spontaneous cast. You're not really the storyteller this time.

3. **Rejection is hard to take.** You cannot choose everyone, right? If you do no one will be watching. It is hard on the kids who don't make the cut.

4. **There's a fair amount of advance work**. You will need to make a script of the story for yourself, create simple lines for

the characters, and quickly rehearse them. Adapting this way can take time.

Make It Work for You

1. **Do your homework.** Make sure you have chosen a very simple story with lots of possible parts.

2. **Ask for help.** Grab an extra staff person, or an adult from the crowd to help line folks up, get them off, or whisper the missing line.

3. **Use sound effects.** Braying donkeys and clucking chickens make it possible for even the youngest to shine. And the flock can be as large or as small as is useful.

4. **Be sure to recruit adults.** That is, unless it is an all-kid group. If so, then look around carefully to be sure you choose cooperative volunteers from all ages and all cultures represented. This can mean fast footwork, but a group of kids in the library usually means a visit from a class. A school visit means staff are present. Good. Let the teacher help you select.

5. **Go crazy.** Might as well use some small props for the characters. Try some little half-masks for each animal.

NOTE

In an unpublished study done in 2000 in six Las Vegas schools, Kendall told one participation story and one nonparticipation story to six in-school, primary grade audiences (total audience just over 1,400). All stories were original stories. None were familiar to the various audiences. He varied both the stories and the order in which they were told. He asked the teachers not to discuss the stories with their students, to wait one day, and to then ask students, without discussion, to draw one picture from one of the two stories (nominally as part of a thank-you letter).

Over one-third of the teachers followed through as asked. Of the 420 pictures Kendall received, three-quarters were from the story in which students did *not* have assigned participation lines. A third of the pictures from the participation stories were of the children saying their lines. When they were given assigned participation lines, their memory of their participation overshadowed their memory of the story.

CHAPTER 12

Let the Stories Roll!

Now that you are on the way to becoming a seasoned storyteller, it is time to develop more ways to incorporate stories into your work and into the library's programs. Doing so will keep you fresh and your enthusiasm intact. The suggestions below are just that, suggestions. We know you'll develop better ones because you know your system and its available resources. That includes the level of interest and support you may anticipate from your administration. If you are fortunate enough to have an administrator who nudged YOU into storytelling—great, thank your lucky stars. The next best thing is someone who is neither for nor against, someone who allows you to make a persuasive case for your plans. Let's hope one of these two situations reflects yours. If not, let's hope no one will discourage you, since changing negative attitudes always adds a layer of work.

Choose what pleases you; ignore what doesn't apply.

WHERE TO START

Start with simple, low-cost activities within your own system, or single library.

Host a monthly story-sharing meeting for interested staff. Encourage folks to tell, but don't make it mandatory, so that they can come and listen until they are emboldened to try. This kind of thing should be open to everyone, not just librarians. It is wise to have a rotating host, so that you're not always the one ripping open the bags of cookies and heating the water for the chaste herbal teas. If your own library is too small to support such an undertaking, then seek out staff in neighboring libraries to join you.

Set up a simple listserv to encourage story swapping, reviews of stories told, and collections used. It is particularly useful to get war stories, that is, accounts of what worked and what didn't. This should be anecdotal and easygoing, with the emphasis on beginners. No lecturing allowed.

Expand the story-swapping group if yours works well. You can put a notice in the usual outlets and invite the public in. Since it will be ongoing, say every month, then a modest success suffices in the beginning. This is different from a library program of themed story collecting such as reminiscences from World War II (see below). This is simply a story-sharing group for listeners and tellers alike. You will likely encounter the usual response: "What exactly *is* this?" Be prepared to answer that question by having some stories of your own to share and thus demonstrate "what it is."

SPECIAL PROGRAMS

You can formalize the idea of story sharing by hosting a program for the public (include staff) that is organized around a single sort of story or idea (theme). Here are some simple ones: stories from veterans of wars, collection of local history tales, grandchildren soliciting stories from grandparents, recipes and the stories behind them (with the possibility of publishing the findings.) You can reinforce the importance of traditional tales by developing a theme and then presenting some related folktales that you tell.

This is a little more difficult than eliciting personal or family tales, but worth doing. Your community's culture and identity will suggest possibilities. Most of these programs are tailor-made for collaboration with other organizations. The local quilting group can partner with needle tales or reminiscences; the local historian or curator can help with stories about your community or region. You'll think of others. Storytelling festival organizers are often interested in these partnerships. Jim May, a fine storyteller from Illinois, encouraged stories from local seniors by presenting the opportunity at his local library.

MORE AMBITIOUS IDEAS

1. **Begin with a bang.** This one is designed to get your colleagues to buy in at the beginning. Hire a really good storytelling educator for a one-time-only workshop for staff. (You could invite the public as well, of course.) We have found that it is more effective to allot a long morning at least. We know this idea presents all sorts of issues, chief among them a scheduling challenge. Still, we think the effort is worth it. Administrative support and encouragement are essential here. The library director needs to get behind this and attend.

   The benefits are considerable. The whole staff sees firsthand what storytelling is, how much fun it can be, and how affecting the tales are for everyone. Staff members get to practice in a safe environment, and everyone is an equal partner. Libraries are, as we librarians know all too well, hierarchical by nature. For instance, a young, inexperienced librarian can find herself in charge of a staff with years of experience. In this workshop everyone has stories to tell.

2. **Storytelling kickoff.** While a day of learning is inherently valuable, you can extend the value by using the workshop day as a kickoff for storytelling in your library. This requires work, coordination, brainstorming, cross-departmental cooperation, and good PR. That's lots of work. Mounting this kind of programmatic machine suggests that you might as well offer a lot of opportunities for telling and listening, since the work will be no more if you do. Here are some ideas:

- Invite groups to tell their particular sorts of tales. The Tejas Storytelling Festival decided to invite local lawyers from Denton, Texas, to the festival to tell their stories. It was a rousing success, and certainly one of the best-attended events of the weekend. Lawyers use stories all the time, so it wasn't difficult to find some to step up.

- Send library-storytellers out into the community to offer short programs of tales. The traditional clubs and service organizations are always looking for speakers, so contact the Rotary, the Chamber of Commerce, etc.

Use these or similar ideas as organizing themes during your storytelling month, or week . . . or even day.

3. **Produce your own library storytelling festival.** There are several models, including the King County Library System Storyfest International. That one presents professional storytellers, but you can also use staff and community storytellers to good effect. The renaissance of storytelling has produced festivals and events and a related wealth of information about planning storytelling events. You can also ring up the nearest storytelling festival's director and get some good advice. This project requires lots of work, make no mistake. It also requires a budget and administrative support.

You can combine an invited teller or two with community storytelling and workshops. Libraries have partnered with arts organizations to produce many storytelling events. A quick Web search or a call to the National Storytelling Network (NSN) will yield lots of ideas, referrals, information, and examples.

If you decide to hire a professional teller, then get your money's worth. Hustle these folks out into the community, and offer them as motivational speakers to city councils, clubs, and groups. Of course, once you've got a trained, motivated, confident group of staff storytellers, they can do it as well.

KEEP ON KEEPING ON

Consider treating the nearest storytelling festival as an opportunity for an in-service training for your staff. It requires a budget for registration, but that is money well spent if staff members come back revved up and ready to tell.

Set up a professional collection of tales, sourcebooks, and guides for staff to use. Yes, this will create a small dent in the collection development budget, but an enterprise is only as good as its tools.

The most important investment is a philosophical one. If you can reach system consensus about the importance of storytelling as a part of library service, then it is easier to create opportunities for professional development, programmatic applications, and a broad, flexible definition.

Do what libraries are already good at doing: finding the answer or the resource. Librarians who are knowledgeable about storytelling and stories—or interested in becoming so—can act as a very effective resource. Bibliographic support for storytelling can be a make-or-break activity. When a staff storyteller can quickly put her finger on a brief list of stories to choose from, the chances are that she will find a good one, learn it, and tell it with dispatch. Interested staff can collaborate on lists of stories that work for holidays, outreach presentations, particular ages or themes, really any sort of occasion. Of course, there are books that have anticipated this need, but we have a less formal approach in mind. Just a quick list of, say, fifteen to twenty stories at the ready that are easy to get to and easy to use. Remember to include several *very* short stories (one to three minutes long).

A REALLY big idea is to commit to storytelling as an essential library service by identifying a staff person as the primary resource. This means formalizing your intention by putting storytelling activities, support, education, and training in the job description. This is a bold, even presumptuous idea, we know, since libraries are chronically underfunded and understaffed. However, when one person is charged with a professional storytelling concentration, the commitment to storytelling is made manifest in his or her work. He or she can train, of course, but also provide stories to tell, create programs for telling them, and, best of all, establish a continuous kind of encouragement that mitigates against "The Predictable Disappearance of the Really Good, Well-Meaning Idea."

Appendix 1

The Structure of Stories

Most of the time you'll tell tested, proven stories. You'll get them out of published books. You won't have to evaluate the effectiveness of the story's structure. Collectors, authors, editors, and past tellers have done that for you. You'll focus on learning and telling.

However, it's good to consider the essential elements of a story that you'll need to get across to your audience. Over the past fifteen years, cognitive research has confirmed what tellers and writers have known intuitively for centuries: the human mind is literally hardwired to interpret information and experience in a specific story form, and in accordance with a specific story structure. Humans make sense out of what they see and hear by using story structure to create meaning and understanding.

This is certainly our belief and our observation from, collectively, fifty years of storytelling experience. It is also the consistent conclusion of recent science research. (See the endnote for a list of some of these studies.) These, and thirty other research studies, have all confirmed that the human brain receives, interprets, processes, understands, relates to, creates meaning from, remembers, and recalls experience and information by using specific internal mental story maps.

The studies have shown that the power and allure of stories emanates from five elements of information around which stories are constructed. These five elements form the informational core of a story.

Three reasons why it's worth your while to understand these elements:

1. Some aspects of a story are more crucial to listeners than others. Knowing the anatomy of stories saves you time.

2. The more you understand the core elements of a story, the easier it is to learn the story and the more comfortably you'll tell it.

3. Recognizing these elements will help you identify stories that will be easy for you to learn and tell.

WHAT *IS* A STORY?

We find that story structural analysis using these five elements is useful. It is a valuable way to look at stories, to assess why they work—or don't work—for you, to deepen your understanding of narrative, and to facilitate your storytelling.

So what are these five essential elements of stories? A story is a unique and specific narrative structure that includes a sense of completeness. Stories have a beginning point and a defined ending point. They come to resolution.

Stories pass on wisdom, experience, information, and facts. Stories shape beliefs and values. They are the building blocks of knowledge, the foundation of memory and learning. Stories model effective use of language. They create empathy, provide perspectives though which we can view other times and other worlds, and connect us with the deepest aspects of our humanity. Stories link past, present, and future by teaching us to use past experience to anticipate the possible future consequences of our present actions.

But these are *characteristics* of a story. What *is* a story?

Character

All stories are about *characters*. Story events happen to characters.

Character and plot are conjoined twins, really, for we can't have a story without them. Here, the word character includes both the existence of the physical entity and the descriptive detail provided in the story so that listeners will be able to see, identify, and understand the character.

Beginning tellers may be misled or confused when comparing the abundant character detail lavished on characters populating modern literary stories to the relative paucity of character detail explicitly provided in traditional tales. The frugality of character detail in folktales is not an oversight, but a clever design characteristic. The characters are often predictable, even stereotypical, so that the listener can quickly identify the character's place and purpose in the story. No time is wasted. Rather than breaking the norm with unexpected, quirky, even unique combinations of character traits, the characters in folktales *are* the norm. That, in large part, is their value and appeal.

Coyote is the trickster from the Southwestern United States and Mexico. There isn't a lot of subtlety and nuance. He is who he is: a trickster who lives by his wits and gets in and out of trouble with delicious regularity. He is complex, but not presented with complicated character description and development. For that, we need to schedule a visit with the fictional giants.

The large number of traditional characters who are neither admirable nor appealing sometimes surprises fledgling storytellers. They're useful, though, for they often embody an undesirable trait: greed, avarice, cruelty, and presumption, among many others. Thus, the main character may be the very one who teaches by negative example or by transformation.

A caution. These characters, like their stories, come from, and represent, specific cultures. For the most part, we are not members of those cultures, and certainly are not from the period when the story was collected. That means we have to work a bit to discover the character's significance. It won't always be obvious from the story's text without a basic understanding of the culture.

Intent

Interesting characters don't ramble through stories for no reason. They are always after something. What a character is after in a story is called a *goal*. Goals can shift during a story. Characters can be stuck between two opposing goals. But characters, like real people, always have a reason for what they do.

Every story is about the goal of the main character. An example: *Once there was a girl named Mary who wanted some ice cream.* That one sentence presents a character and a goal. We already know how the story will end: we'll find out if Mary gets her ice cream or not. (Stories end when the main character's goal is resolved.) We will also use that goal to establish the point and purpose to every action and event in the story.

In order for this goal to propel a character through a story's dangers, trials, and tribulations (the plot), the goal must be important to that character. What makes the goal important is called a *motive*. The more important the goal (the bigger the motive), the more suspenseful and intriguing the story. Together, goal and motive create a character's intent.

Conflicts and Problems

Conflicts and problems are the obstacles that a character must contend with to reach a goal. Obstacles can be internal (fears, conflicting wants, ignorance, beliefs, etc.) or external. External obstacles can either be problems (It's too hot. It's too far. There's a mountain to cross.) or conflicts (a troll, an evil wizard, a dragon, etc.).

The antagonist is of great importance to a story, as that being represents the greatest single conflict a main character will have to face. Everyone loves to hate a good antagonist. The more powerful and ruthless the antagonist, the more listeners root for the main character. Certainly a character can be his or her own worst enemy—one's own antagonist. The best fighting is often against oneself.

Conflicts and problems create two things listeners care about a lot: *risk and danger*. *Risk* represents the likelihood that something will go wrong. *Danger* is the consequence (what happens) to a story character when something does go wrong. Excitement does not come from *what* happens in a story (the action). It comes from knowing what *could* happen—the risk and danger created by the conflicts that the main character must face.

Struggles (Plot)

Struggles are what a character does (the action, the plot) to overcome obstacles and reach a goal. Characters must do something. Listeners don't want it to be easy for story characters. The more characters *struggle*—internally and externally—the more gripping the story is. Plot sequences must follow some logic, some understandable pattern—temporal sequencing, cause-and-effect sequencing, etc. Listeners rely on the plot to guide them through events that unfold around characters in a story.

Details

A few key sensory details about the characters, settings, actions, and objects make a story seem real and vivid to listeners. Story details make it possible for listeners to visualize a story in their minds.

These five elements form the underpinning of successful stories. If you see them clearly as you read a story, it will make it easier for you to learn the story and will save you precious time.

An example will help clarify these elements and their role in a story: Once there was an emperor (character) who loved clothes so much that he spent all his money on them (character trait). He was vain and obsessed with having the finest clothes in the land. (Another character trait—in this case an internal character flaw. We assume that significant flaws will eventually get story characters in trouble.)

When the emperor heard of a new and wondrous—indeed, magic—material he insisted on having a robe made from it (goal). This robe would be the finest robe in the land (motive) and would—because of its magic properties—allow the king to tell which of his ministers were fools (motive). But the weavers were liars and cheats (conflict), and the emperor's ministers lacked the courage to tell him the truth (problem).

How will the story end? We must resolve the goal of the main character. So we need the sequence of events that leads to our discovery of whether or not the emperor gets his new clothes. (He does.) We also want to know how he feels about his new robes and are quite pleased when the truth creates great consternation for the emperor and his ministers.

Stories end when the main character resolves—one way or the other—his or her primary goal. Not *reaches*, but *resolves*. Yes, a character can have multiple goals, some physical and tangible, others internal; some will be well known to the character and listeners, some may be hidden until late in the story. Still, the story will reach its end when the character's primary goal is resolved.

What's still missing?

- **Character traits.** After this abbreviated summary of the story, we need a bit more information about the two thieving weavers and a dash more about the emperor in order to ensure that listeners will care whether the emperor gets his comeuppance or the weavers get away with their dastardly scheme. We can't picture these characters as individuals in our minds yet. While it is true that many folktales intentionally contain few character details so that readers can overlay their own images on those unspecified forms, even these tales must contain *just enough* character detail to allow readers to both visualize and care about the story's characters.

- **Struggles.** We don't know yet what the emperor, his ministers, or the weavers actually *do* in the story.

- **Details.** We can't see the character, settings, events, and objects of the story yet because we have added no details.

Those are the five essential elements in action. Knowing these essential elements will always bring you back on track and make sure that you deliver the essential story to your listeners.

NOTE

We have collected more than 100 books, articles, and papers reporting on research that confirm both the concept that humans interpret and create meaning through mental story mapping and the story structure presented in this chapter. A few of the more prominent in this prestigious list are: Ambruseter et al. (1987), Bransford and Brown (2000), Bransford and Stein (1993), Bruner (1990 and 1987), Denning (2001), Egan (1997), Gopnik, *et al* (1999), Kotulak (1999), Mallan (1997), Pinker (2000 and 1997), Ricoeur (1984), Schank (1990), Tannen (1999), and Turner (1996). See the Bibliography for full listings of these publications.

Appendix 2

Who Says Storytelling Is Worthwhile?

Some storytelling research has been mentioned in the various chapters of this book. Additional selected studies and their central themes are presented here. We do not intend this discussion to be an exhaustive review of the available quantitative and qualitative research literature. That would fill its own book. View this appendix not as a balanced meal, but as a sample of tantalizing morsels that hint at the bounty of research that awaits the hungry traveler.

DOES STORYTELLING WORK?

Many studies have examined the effects of storytelling. As far back as 1988, Cliatt and Shaw concluded that, "the relationship of storytelling and successful children's literacy development is well established." Their study showed that "Children learn and internalize story structure from a diet of told and read stories" and that this process enhanced children's development of language and logic skills.

Kendall has collected more than 1,850 anecdotal reports of the use of stories and storytelling (mostly from teachers, librarians, and other storytellers). While he solicited any and all experiences with the use of stories and storytelling, 100 percent—that's each and every one—of these 1,850 anecdotal reports claim that stories and storytelling were an effective and engaging addition to their programs that enthused and engaged listeners and efficiently taught essential story content. Storytelling works.

Haven has also collected more than 150 research-based studies (both quantitative and qualitative) that assessed the effectiveness of stories and storytelling. Since many of these studies were themselves reviews of a collection of other studies, these 150 studies contain the results of more than 600 separate research efforts. *None* reported that stories or storytelling were ineffective, or even that stories and storytelling were less effective than available alternatives included in the studies. Again, 100 percent of the available studies supported the value of stories and storytelling. That result is, in itself, amazing.

Snow and Burns (1998) concluded their examination of a number of previous studies by saying: "Recently the efficacy of early reading and storytelling exposure has been scientifically validated. It has been shown to work (to develop language skills)." .Similarly, Schank (1990) used his research to show that, "Storytelling has demonstrable, measurable, positive, and irreplaceable value in teaching."

In a more recent study, Mello (2001) reported on ten studies of elementary students including pre- and post-interviews and writing sample analysis. Each of the research reports she studied documented that storytelling enhanced literacy. She concluded that, "storytelling was an effective learning tool that linked literature to content and experience."

O'Neill, Peare, and Pick (2004) studied the storytelling ability of preschool students in Ontario, Canada, and found good correlation between early storytelling skills and later math abilities. O'Neill suggests that time spent on early storytelling skill development in preschool years improves math skill upon entering school. More important, this study establishes storytelling skill as both predating, and as precursor for, logical thinking development.

As a small section of his unpublished doctoral work, Janner (1997) conducted an interesting study with four fourth-grade classrooms. He delivered the same story to each class. To one, he read the story. He gave copies of the story to one class and had students read it. He showed a video of the story to one class, and he told the story to the final class. One month later he interviewed selected students from each class to see how the media of delivery affected their retained images of the story.

The students who most accurately recalled the story and its images came from the class that had seen the video. However, the students who were the most enthusiastic and excited about their recollection of the story, who held the most vivid and expansive images of the story, and who were best able to verbalize their memory (and version) of the story were those from the class to whom he *told* the story.

Clearly, this was a small study that contained many uncontrolled variables. Still, its conclusion are inescapable and dramatic. Storytelling creates excitement, enthusiasm, and more detailed and expansive images in the mind of the listener than does the same story delivered in other ways.

Chang (2006), a regional director of education for Taiwan, stated, "Living in a highly competitive environment places great pressure on the efficiency and effectiveness of every moment spent at school. I am convinced that stories hold a solution. They teach valuable language skills, effectively teach facts and concepts, and are finally something fun for our students to do."

Schank (1990), and later Dalkir and Wiseman (2004), concluded that storytelling is not only effective at conveying factual and conceptual information, but is also most effective at communicating tacit knowledge, "that which is difficult to articulate, to render tangible in some form." They included in this category values, beliefs, attitudes, cultural norms, etc.

In his 1989 study, Coles showed that stories connect character truth with scientific truth. The dominance of characters in stories and storytelling provides context, empathy, and relevance for the scientific material by using characters to explain intention, action, struggles, and reaction around factual information. Characters represent surrogate models for the reader and allow the reader to interpret and understand content and, thus, to create meaning. Similarly, Howard (1991) concluded that "science *is* a form of storytelling. Science meaning is constructed and conveyed through storytelling." He proposed that story elements create context and relevance that provide a way for the reader to understand and to create meaning from the content material they read.

The success of storytelling is not limited to educational and science venues. The same results were found in studies of organizations. Industry surveys conducted by Cooper (1997) concluded that, "In fact, researchers have found that potential employers want their employees to have mastered two aspects of literacy often omitted from school curricula: listening and speaking."

Boyce (1996) and Kahan (2001) conducted an extensive reviews of research on organizational story and storytelling. All of these studies viewed stories as an effective and valuable—even essential and unavoidable—part of every organization. Kahan stated, "Storytelling is increasingly seen as an important tool for communicating explicit and especially tacit knowledge—not just information, but know-how."

Denning (2001) reported that, "Time after time, when faced with the task of persuading a group of manages or front-line staff in a large organization to get enthusiastic about a major change, storytelling was the only thing that worked."

WHY AND HOW DOES STORYTELLING WORK?

Medical technological advancements over the past decade have resulted in vast amounts of new information emanating from the fields of neurolinguistics, neurobiology, cognitive research, and developmental psychology. A tiny mound of that mountain is mentioned here.

Mallan (1997) concluded that, "Stories differ from other narratives (arguments, scientific reports, articles) in that they orient our feelings and attitudes about the story content." His research showed that this emotional engagement is why information presented in the structure of a story is more easily remembered. He added that, "*Told* stories have the advantage of making the story accessible to all levels of reading proficiency."

Mello (2001) suggested that storytelling creates empathy for tellers and for a story's main characters and that this empathy significantly contributed to the power and effectiveness of storytelling.

In reporting research conducted with infants and very young children, Bransford and Brown (2000) stated that, "Young infants learn to pay attention to the features of speech and storytelling, such as intonation and rhythm, that help them obtain critical information about language and meaning." They also reported that, "There appear to be separate brain areas that specialize in subtasks such as hearing words (spoken language recognition), seeing words (reading), speaking words (speech), and generating words (thinking with language)." Bransford suspected that early oral language activity (storytelling and story listening) was particularly important for the development of these various centers.

In her 1995 study, Engle asked, "How is it that children, born with no language, can develop the rudiments of storytelling in the first three years of life?" She concluded that "children learn storytelling many years before they master logic, persuasion, writing, and other forms of information delivery."

Egan (1997) pointed out that every developing civilization knew and relied on story and storytelling long before logic, long before writing. "There have been no preliterate groups who did not develop oral myth and folk story. Why should these particular stories be culturally universal?" He and many others concluded that human reliance on oral storytelling and on the traditional forms of myth and folktale relate to what neurobiologists have recently confirmed about brain structure. Human minds are hardwired to interpret and understand information and experience in story form.

Humans are predisposed to favor and to rely on the form of story and the process of storytelling.

Remember, this is just a small sampling, a mere taste. Indulge. Research delights are available to bolster your position that storytelling is an important offering for your library!

Appendix 3

Copyright and You

A copyright is a bundle of five rights granted by U.S. law to the creator of any intellectual material—such as a story. Under current U.S. law, the creator does not have to do anything to obtain these exclusive rights. Creators get them automatically when they create and fix their creations in any tangible form (write it down; say it into a tape recorder, etc.). The copyright holder no longer even needs to place a copyright notification (© Kendall Haven, 2005) on a copy of the work to protect the copyright.

There are five specific rights that we grant exclusively to an author in this bundle of rights. These are the exclusive right to publish the work, to copy the work, to create derivative copies of the work (to change it), to promote the work, and to perform it. That last one is where storytellers can run afoul of the copyright laws.

What can authors copyright? Anything original in a book they publish—but only what is original to them. You will never know what is (and is not) protected by copyright by looking at the copyright notification on a book. There are many collections of folk tales that display a general copyright protection notice in which the only thing actually being copyrighted is the specific typeface and layout being used to present the stories—not the stories themselves.

How can you tell if a story (or even parts of a story) you want to tell is covered by a copyright? Unfortunately, it's often extremely difficult to tell. The story you pull from your library shelves might *look* like an original picture book with a current author, and yet the copyright may only cover the illustrations. The copyright notice does not have to spell out what exactly is (and is not) being protected. As a storyteller's rule of thumb, if you can find three versions of the same story in different source books, you are free and clear to tell it without seeking anyone's permission.

How long do copyrights last? Well, it depends. The U.S. copyright laws have changed several times, and the length of a copyright depends on the year of publication. In general, most recently published books come with a copyright that lasts a maximum of the life of the author plus fifty years.

How does copyright law affect you and your storytelling? If you tell folktales, fairy tales, traditional tales, myths or legends (as well as many tall tales), it doesn't. Those are the stories that, with rare exception, are in the public domain and are fair for all of us to use and tell to our heart's content. If, however, you choose to tell literary tales, you *will* bump against copyright infringement.

Most authors are thrilled to have librarians use their books during booktalks and storytelling sessions. Most. But not all. Technically, you may not even read a copyrighted storybook to your weekly story time crowd without expressed permission from the copyright holder. However, librarians do it all the time. Reading an entire story is *not* covered by the "fair use" exclusion to the copyright laws that allows you to extract and present a small portion of a copyrighted work during scholarly review, critique, or parody or to make one copy of a copyright-protected story for your own use.

Neither of us can conceive of an author trying to claim that your telling his or her story harmed that author's monetary interest in the work or reduced in any way his or her income from it. (The criteria by which authors can bring monetary suit against you for telling it.) Neither of us can imagine an author trying to stop you from reading or telling his or her published story in your library. We can't possibly imagine it. It would make no sense since librarians are doing the author an honor and are providing valuable marketing by presenting the tale. Still, it *could* happen.

How can you protect yourself? Simple. Tell stories from the wealth of public domain stories and stories you know other librarian tellers have successfully told without author retribution. If they didn't get in trouble, neither will you. When you stretch beyond that cover, we feel obligated to say that the safest thing to do is to write (or e-mail) the author and ask permission to tell the story in your library. Every sensible author will gladly say, "Yes." If he or she says, "no," then spread the word. As we said, we can't imagine any author refusing such permission.

We don't think you need to stay up nights fretting over copyright. However, it is good to be aware of it. Further, it's a good policy for you to support these rights since they are what make it possible for authors to create and share their wonderful works.

Appendix 4

Definitions of Traditional Tales

The following definitions of the types of traditional tales are taken from *Webster's Third New International Dictionary of the English Language, Unabridged* (Phillip Babcock Gove, ed. Springfield, MA: Merriam-Webster, Inc., 1981).

Anecdote: A short narrative of interesting, amusing, or curious incidents often biographical and generally characterized by human interest.

Epic: A long narrative poem recounting the deeds of a legendary or historical hero.

Fable: A narration intended to enforce some universal truth or precept, especially one in which animals and even inanimate objects talk and act as human beings.

Fairy tale: A narrative containing supernatural or improbable events, scenes, or personages and often having a whimsical, satirical, or moralistic character.

Folktale: A tale circulated by word of mouth among the common people, especially a tale characteristically anonymous and timeless.

Legend: A story coming down from the past popularly regarded as historical, although not entirely verifiable.

Myth: A story that is usually of unknown origin, and at least partly traditional, that ostensibly relates historical events, usually of such a character as to explain some practice, belief, institution, or natural phenomenon that is especially associated with religious rites and beliefs.

Bibliography

We offer this bibliography with special thanks to Infopeople, a company that provides training and instruction for library staffs across California. Their invention, responsiveness, and organization make them an unrivaled model. They have graciously allowed us to include many of the sections of this bibliography.

REFERENCES: WORKS CITED IN THIS BOOK

Ambruster, B., et al. (1987). "Does Text Structure/Summarization Instruction Facilitate Learning from Expository Text?" *Reading Research Quarterly* 22: 331–346.

Boyce, M. (1996). "Organizational Story and Storytelling: A Critical Review." *Journal of Organizational Change Management* 9 (5): 5–26.

Bransford, J., and A. Brown, eds. (2000). *How People Learn.* Washington, DC: National Academy Press.

Bransford, J., and B. Stein. (1993). *The Ideal Problem Solver.*, 2d ed. New York: Freeman.

Bruner, J. (1986). *Actual Minds, Possible Worlds.* Cambridge, MA: Harvard University Press.

———. (1987). "Life as Narrative." *Social Research* 54: 11–32.

———. (1990). *Acts of Meaning.* Cambridge, MA: Harvard University Press.

———. (1992). "The Narrative Construction of Reality." In *Piaget's Theory: Prospects and Possibilities,* edited by H Beilin and P. Pufall, 229–248. ' Hillsdale, NJ: Lawrence Erlbaum.

Cliatt, M., and J. Shaw. (1988). "The Storytime Exchange: Ways to Enhance It." *Childhood Education* 64 (5): 293–298.

Coles, Robert. (1989). *The Call of Stories.* Boston: Houghton-Mifflin.

Cooper, J. (1997). *Literacy: Helping Children Construct Meaning.* Boston: Houghton Mifflin.

Dalkir, K., and E. Wiseman. (2004). "Organizational Storytelling and Knowledge Management: A Survey." *Storytelling, Self, Society* 1 (1, Fall): 57–73.

Denning, S. (2001). *The Springboard: How Storytelling Ignites Action in Knowledge-Era Organizations.* Boston: Butterworth-Heinemann.

Egan, K. (1997). *The Educated Mind: How Cognitive Tools Shape Our Understanding.* Chicago: University of Chicago Press.

Engle, S. (1995). *The Stories Children Tell: Making Sense of the Narratives of Childhood.* New York: Freeman.

Fisher, W. (1987). *Human Communications as Narration: Toward a Philosophy of Reason, Value, and Action*. Columbia: University of South Carolina Press.

———. (1994). "Narrative as a Human Communications Paradigm: The Case of Public Moral Argument." *Communications Monograph* 51: 1–20.

Gopnik, A., et al. (1999). *The Scientist in the Crib*. New York: HarperPerennial.

Haven, K. (2004) *Get It Write!*. Portsmouth, NH: Teacher Ideas Press.

Howard, G. (1991). "Culture Takes: A Narrative Approach to Thinking, Cross-Cultural Psychology, and Psychotherapy." *American Psychologist* 47 (3, March): 187–197.

Janner, B. (1997). *The Psychological Effects of Alternate Means of Mass Communication*. Ph.D. dissertation, Ann Arbor, University of Michigan.

Kahan, S. (2001). "Bringing Us Back to Life: Storytelling and the Modern Organization." *Information Outlook* 5 (5): 26–29.

Kotulak, R. (1999). *Inside the Brain: Revolutionary Discoveries of How the Mind Works*. Kansas City: Andrews McNeal.

Mallan, Kerry. (1997). "Storytelling in the School Curriculum." *Educational Practice & Theory* 19 (1): 75–82.

Mello, R. (2001). "Building Bridges: How Storytelling Influences Teacher/Student Relationships." In *Proceedings, Storytelling in the Americas Conference*. St Catherine, ON: Brooks University Press.

O'Neill, D., M. Pearce, and J. Pick. (2004). "Predictive Relations Between Aspects of Preschool Children's Narratives and Performance on the Peabody Individualized Achievement Test—Revised: Evidence of a Relation Between Early Narrative and Later Mathematical Ability." *First Language* 24 (June): 149–183.

Pinker, S. (1997). *How the Mind Works*. New York: W. W. Norton.

———. (2000). *The Language Instinct*. New York: Perennial Classic.

Ricoeur, Paul. (1984). *Time and Narrative*. Chicago: University of Chicago Press.

Schank, R. (1990). *Tell Me a Story*. New York: Charles Scribner's Sons.

Shank, R., and R. Abelson. 91995). "Knowledge and Memory: The Real Story." In *Knowledge and Memory: The Real Story,* edited by R. Wyer Jr., 1–85. Hillsdale, NJ: Erlbaum.

Snow, C., and M. Burns, eds. (1998). *Preventing Reading Difficulties in Young Children*. Washington, DC: National Research Council and National Academy Press.

Tannen, D. (1999). *Talking Voices: Repetition, Dialogue, and Imagery in Conversational Discourse*. New York: Cambridge University Press.

Turner, M. (1996). *The Literary Mind: The Origins of Thought and Language*. New York: Oxford University Press.

STORYTELLING ADVICE, APPROACHES, THEORY, AND STORIES

These titles contain both tales and commentary on storytelling. Suggestions include how to work with a particular group; specific genres; and general advice about choosing, learning, and telling stories.

Baker, Agusta, and Ellin Greene. "Storytelling: Preparation and Presentation," *School Library Journal* (March 1978): 93–97.

Barton, Bob. *Tell Me Another.* New York: Heinemann, 1986.

Birch, Carol, and Melissa Heckler, eds. *Who Says: Essays on Pivotal Issues in Contemporary Storytelling.* Little Rock, AR: August House Publishers, 1998.

Breneman, Lucille, and Bren Breneman. *Once Upon a Time: A Storytelling Handbook.* Chicago: Nelson-Hall, 1983.

Browne, M. Neil, and Stuart Keeley. *Asking the Right Questions.* Englewood Cliffs, NJ: Prentice Hall, Inc., 1981.

Burrell, Arthur. *A Guide to Story Telling.* London: Sir Isaac Pitman & Sons, 1946.

Carlson, Bernice Wells. *Listen! And Help Tell the Story.* Nashville, TN: Abington, 1965.

Coles, Robert. *The Call to Stories: Teaching and the Moral Imagination.* Boston: Houghton Mifflin, 1989.

Collins, Rives, and Pamela Cooper. *Look What Happened to Frog: Storytelling in Education.* Cambridge, England: Gorsuch Scarisbrick, 1992.

Colwell, Eileen. *Storytelling.* London: Bodley Head, 1983.

———. *The Magic Umbrella and other Stories for Telling: With Notes on How to Tell Them.* Philadelphia: McKay, 1976.

Cook, Elizabeth. *The Ordinary and the Fabulous.* 2d ed. with addendum. Cambridge, England: Cambridge University Press, 1978.

Dailey, Shiela. *Putting the World in a Nutshell: The Art of the Formula Tale.* New York: H. W. Wilson, 1994.

De Vos, Gail. *Storytelling for Young Adults: Techniques and Treasury.* Englewood, CO: Libraries Unlimited, 1991.

Dorson, Richard. M., ed. *Folklore and Folklife.* Chicago: University of Chicago Press, 1972.

Egan, Kieran. *Teaching as Storytelling.* Chicago: University of Chicago Press, 1989.

Greene, Ellin. *Storytelling: Art and Technique.* New York: Bowker, 1996.

Hamilton, Martha, and Mitch Weiss. *Children Tell Stories: A Teaching Guide.* Katonah, NY: Richard Owen Publications, 1990.

Haven, Kendall. *Super Simple Storytelling*. Englewood, CO: Libraries Unlimited, 2001.

Holt, David, and Bill Mooney, eds. *Ready-To-Tell Tales: Surefire Stories from America's Favorite Storytellers*. Little Rock, AR: August House Publishers, 1994.

Lane, Marcia. *Picturing the Rose :A Way of Looking at Fairy Tales*. New York: H. W. Wilson, 1994.

Livo, Norma, and Sandra A. Rietz. *Storytelling: Process and Practice*. Littleton, CO: Libraries Unlimited, 1986.

Luthi, Max. *Once Upon a Time: On the Nature of Fairy Tales*. Bloomington: Indiana University Press, 1976.

MacDonald, Margaret Read. *The Storyteller's Start-Up Book: Finding, Learning, Performing and Using Folktales*. Little Rock, AR: August House, 1993.

———. *Traditional Storytelling Today: An International Sourcebook*. New York: Fitzroy Dearborn, 1999.

Miller, Teresa. *Joining In: An Anthology of Audience Participation Tales and How to Tell Them*. Sommerville, MA: Yellow Moon, 1988.

Mooney, Bill, and David Holt. *More Ready-to-Tell Tales from Around the World*. Little Rock, AR: August House Publishers,2002.

———. *The Storyteller's Guide*. Little Rock, AR: August House Publishers, 1997.

Mooney, Bill, and David Holt, eds. *The Storyteller's Guide: Storytellers Share Advice for the Classroom, Boardroom, Showroom, Podium, Pulpit, and Center Stage*. Little Rock, AR: August House Publishers, 1996.

Norfolk, Bobby, and Sherry Norfolk. *The Moral of the Story: Folktales for Character Development*. Little Rock, AR: August House Publishers, 1999.

Pellowski, Anne. *The Family Storytelling Handbook*. Little Rock, AR: August House, 1995.

Rydell, Katy, ed. *A Beginner's Guide to Storytelling*. Jonesborough, TN: National Storytelling Network, 2002.

Sawyer, Ruth. *The Way of the Storyteller*. New York: Viking, 1942.

Schimmel, Nancy. *Just Enough to Make a Story: A Sourcebook for Storytelling*. 3d ed. Berkeley, CA: Sisters Choice Press, 1992.

Shedlock, Maria L. *The Art of Storytelling*. Mineola, NY: Dover, 1951.

Stotter, Ruth. *About Story: Writings on Stories and Storytelling 1980–1994*. San Rafael, CA: Stotter Press, 1994.

Trousdale, Ann, Sue Woestehoff, and Marni Schwartz. *Give a Listen; Stories of Storytelling in School*. Urbana, IL: NCTE, 1994.

Zipes, Jack. *The Oxford Companion to Fairy Tales*. New York: Oxford University Press, 2000.

STORYTELLING RESEARCH GUIDES AND COMMENTARY

Aarne, Antti *The Types of the Folk-tale: A Classification and Bibliography.* Translated and enlarged by Stith Thompson. Folklore Communications, no. 184. Helsinki: Suomalainen Tiedeakatemia, 1973.

Ashliman, D. L. *A Guide to Folktales in the English Language.* Westport, CT: Greenwood Press, 1987.

Eastman, Mary Huse, ed. *Index to Fairy Tales, Myths and Legends. Boston:* Boston Book Co., 1915. (See 1926 edition.)

Ireland, Norma Olin. *Index to Fairy Tales 1949–1972: Including Folklore, Legends and Myths in Collections.* Westport, CT: Greenwood Press, 1973. (Continued Eastman's efforts. See later editions.)

Leach, Maria, ed., and Jerome Fried, associate ed. *Funk & Wagnalls Standard Dicionary of Folklore, Mythology and Legends.* New York: Funk & Wagnalls, 1972. (See earlier and later editions.)

MacDonald, Margaret Read. *The Storyteller's Sourcebook: A Subject, title and Motif Index to Folklore Collections for Children.* New York: Neal-Schuman in association with Gale Research, 1982.

MacDonald, Margaret Read, and Brian W. Sturm. *Storyteller's Sourcebook: A Subject, Title, and Motif Index to Folklore Collections for Children, 1983–1999.* Farmington Hills, MI: Gale Research, 2001.

Sierra, Judy. *Storytellers' Research Guide: Folktales, Myths and Legends.* Nashville, TN: Folkprint, 1996.

RELIABLE COLLECTIONS OF TRADITIONAL TALES

Many of the authors listed below have published several works. The two asterisks that follow some of the entries indicate authors with more than one title of interest. Some of the books are out of print.

Abrahams, Roger. *African Folktales.* London: Pantheon, 1983. (From the reliable Pantheon Fairy Tale and Folktale Library. See other examples below.)

Abrahams, Roger D. *Afro-American Folktales.* London: Pantheon, 1985.

Afanasev, Aleksandr. *Russian Fairy Tales.* London: Pantheon, 1945.

Asbjornsen, Peter Christian, and Jorgen Moe. *Popular Tales from the Norse.* Translated by Sir George Webb Nasent. Edinburgh: David Douglas, 1888. (See later version by Asbjornsen, titled *East O' the Sun and West O' the Moon.*)

Asubel, Nathan. *A Treasury of Jewish Folklore.* New York: Crown, 1948.

Bader, Barbara. *Aesop and Company: With Scenes from His Legendary Life.* Boston: Houghton Mifflin, 1991.

Belpre, Pura. *Once in Puerto Rico.* London: Warne, 1973.

Bierhorst, John. ed. *Black Rainbow: Legends of the Incas & Myths of Ancient Peru.* New York: Farrar, Straus & Giroux, 1976.**

———. *Latin American Folktales: Stories from Hispanic and Indian Traditions.* New York: Pantheon, 2000.

Boggs, Ralph. *Three Golden Oranges and Other Spanish Tales.* Mineola, NY: Longmans, 1936. (Dover reissue.)

Briggs, Katharine M. *A Dictionary of British Folk-Tales.* Bloomington: Indiana University Press, 1970.

Bryan, Ashley. *Beat the Story Drum, Pum, Pum.* New York: Atheneum, 1980.

Bushnaq, Inea. *Arab Folktales.* Pantheon, 1986.

Calvino, Italo. *Italian Tales.* New York: Harcourt Brace Jovanovich, 1980.

Chase, Richard. *The* Jack Tales. Boston: Houghton Mifflin, 1943**

Cole, Joanna. *Best-Loved Folktales of the World.* New York: Doubleday, 1982.

Courlander, Harold. *The Hat-Shaking Dance and Other Ashanti Tales from Ghana.* New York: Harcourt, 1957. **

Curtis, Edward. S. *The Girl Who Married a Ghost and Other Tales from North American Indians.* Edited by John Bierhorst. Columbus, OH: Four Winds Press, 1978.

Dalal, Anita. *Myths of Oceania.* New York: Raintree Steck-Vaughn, 2002.

De Vos, Gail. *Storytelling for Young Adults: Techniques and Treasury.* Englewood, CO: Libraries Unlimited, 1991.

Dorson, Richard. *Folktales Told Around the World.* Chicago: University of Chicago Press, 1975.

Durham, Mae. *Tit for Tat and Other Latvian Folk Tales.* New York: Harcourt, Brace and World, 1967.

Erdoes, Richard, and Alphonso Ortiz. *American Indian Myths and Legends.* London: Pantheon, 1984.

Fillmore, Parker. *The Shepherd's Nosegay.* New York: Harcourt, Brace, 1958.

Glassie, Henry. *Irish Folk Tales.* London: Pantheon, 1985.

Griego y Maestas, Jose, and Rudolfo Anaya. *Cuentos: Tales from the Hispanic Southwest*: Based on stories originally collected by Juan B. Rael. Albuquerque: Museum of New Mexico Press, 1980. (Bilingual collection: Griego selected and adapted in Spanish, Anaya retold in English.)

Grimm, Jacob, and Wilhelm Grimm. *Grimm's Fairy Tales for Young and Old.* Translated by Ralph Manheim. Doubleday, 1977. (See also translations by both Jack Zipes and Maria Tatar.)

Hamilton, Virginia. *The People Could Fly: American Black Folktales.* New York: Knopf, 1985. **

Hearn, Lafcadio. *Japanese Fairy Tales.* New York: Liveright, 1953.

Howard, Norman. *The Girl Who Dreamed Only Geese, and Other Tales of the Far North.* New York: Harcourt, Brace, 1997.

Hume, Lotta Carswell. *Favorite Children's Stories from China and Tibet.* North Clarendon, VT: Tuttle, 2000.

Hyde-Chambers, Frederick, and Audrey Hyde Chambers. *Tibetan Folktales.* Boston: Shambhala, 1981.

Jacobs, Joseph. *English Folk and Fairy Tales.* New York: G. P. Putnam's Sons, c. 1898. **

Jaffrey, Madhur. *Seasons of Splendor: Tales, Myths & Legends of India.* New York: Atheneum, 1985.

Jataka Tales. Edited by Nancy DeRoin. Boston: Houghton Mifflin, 1975.

Jewett, Eleanor Myers. *Which Was Witch: Tales of Ghosts and Magic from Korea.* New York: Viking, 1953.

Kendall, Carol. *Sweet and Sour: Tales from China.* New York: Seabury Press, 1979.

Kelsey, Alice Geer. *Once the Hodja.* Philadelphia: McKay, 1943.

Kroeber, Theodora. *The Inland Whale.* Berkeley: University of California Press, 1970.

Lang, Andrew. *The Rainbow Fairy Book: Selections of Outstanding Tales from the Color Fairy Books.* New York: Viking, 1977. (See others: *The Red Fairy Book,* etc.)**

Lester, Julius. *The Knee-High Man and Other Tales.* New York: Dial, 1972.**

Livo, Norma, and Dia Cha. *Folk Stories of the Hmong: Peoples of Laos, Thailand and Vietnam.* Englewood, CO: Libraries Unlimited, 1992.

MacDonald, Margaret Read. *Three-Minute Tales: Stories from Around the World to Tell or Read When Time Is Short.* Little Rock, AR: August House, 2004.

Minard, Rosemary. *Womenfolk and Fairy Tales.* Boston: Houghton Mifflin, 1975.

Nic Leodhas, Sorche. *Heather and Broom: Tales from the Scottish Highlands.* New York: Holt, 1960. **

Perrault, Charles. *Perrault's Complete Fairy Tales.* Translated by A. E. Johnson. New York: Dover, 1969.

Phillip, Neil. *Fairy Tales of Eastern Europe.* New York: Clarion Books, 1991.

Picard, Barbara Leoni. *Tales of Ancient Persia.* New York: Knopf, 1965.

Riorden, James. *Tales from Tartary.* London: Kestrel, 1978. (Volume 2 of Russian Tales series.) **

Sanfield, Steve. *The Feather Merchants and Other Tales of the Fools of Chelm.* London: Orchard, 1991.

Shah, Idries. *World Tales.* New York: Harcourt, Brace, Jovanovich, 1979.

Sierra, Judy. *The Oryx Multicultural Folktale Series: Cinderella.* Phoenix: Oryx Press, 1992. **

Singer, Isaac Bashevis. *When Schlemiel Went to Warsaw and Other Stories.* New York: Farrar, Straus & Giroux, 1986.**

Tashjian, Virginia. *Juba This and Juba That.* Boston: Little, Brown, 1969.

Tatterhood and Other Tales: *Stories of Magic and Adventure.* Ethel Johnston Phelps, Ed. Feminist Press, 1978.**

Uchida, Yoshiko. *The Dancing Teakettle and Other Japanese Folktales*. New York: Scribner, 1965.

Undset, Sigrid. *True and Untrue and Other Norse Tales*. New York: Knopf, 1945.

Vuong, Lynette Dyer. *The Golden Slipper and other Vietnamese Tales*. Boston: Addison-Wesley, 1982.

Walker, Barbara K. *Once There Was and Twice There Wasn't*. Rover Grove, IL: Follett, 1968.

Williamson, Duncan. *The Broonies, Silkies and Fairies: Travelers' Tales of the Other World*. London: Harmony, 1985.

Wolkstein, Diane. *The Magic Orange Tree and Other Haitian Folktales*. New York: Schocken Books, 1980. **

Yeats, William Butler. *Irish Folk Stories and Fairy Tales*. Edited by William Butler Yeats. New York: Grossett & Dunlap, 1972.

Yolen, Jane. *Favorite Folktales from Around the World*. London: Pantheon, 1986.**

FAMILY AND PERSONAL STORIES

Alessi, Jean, and Jan Miller. *Once Upon a Memory: Your Family Tales and Treasures*. Cincinnati, OH: Betterway,1987.

Bands, Ann, ed. *First Person America*. New York: Random House, 1980.

Darden, Norma Jean, and Carole Darden. *Spoonbread and Strawberry Wine: Recipes and Reminiscences of a Family*. Norwell, MA: Anchor Press, 1978.

Davis, Donald. *Telling Your Own Stories*. Little Rock, AR: August House Publishers, 1997.

Dixon, Janice, and Dora Flack. *Preserving Your Past: A Painless Guide to Writing Your Autobiography and Family History*. New York: Doubleday, 1977.

Frazier, Ian. *Family*. New York: Farrar, Straus & Giroux, 1994.

MacDonald, Margaret Read. *Parents Guide to Storytelling: How to Make Up New Stories and Retell Old Favorites*. 2d ed. Little Rock, AR: August House, 2001.

Moore, Robin. *Awakening the Hidden Storyteller: Creating a Family Storytelling Tradition*. Little Rock, AR: August House, 1999.

Norden, Catherine. *The Way We Looked: The Meaning and Magic of Family Photographs*. New York: Lodestar/Dutton, 1983.

Pellowski, Anne. *The Family Storytelling Book*. New York: Macmillan, 1987.

Stone, Elizabeth. *Black Sheep and Kissing Cousins: How Our Family Stories Shape Us*. New York: Random House, 1988.

Winston, Linda. *Keepsakes: Using Family Stories in Elementary Classrooms*. Portsmouth, NH: Heinemann, 1997.

Zeitlin, Steven J., Any J. Kotlin, and Holly Cutting Baker. *A Celebration of American Family Folklore: Tales and Traditions from the Smithsonian Collection*. London: Pantheon, 1982.

PARTICIPATION STORIES

Traditional tales that appear in many collections are listed by title only. We include full citations for literary stories and for retellings of traditional tales that we prefer.

Ask Mr. Bear. Marjory Flack. New York: Macmillan, 1958.

The Banza. Dianne Wolkstein. New York: Dial, 1981.

Big Pumpkin. Erica Silverman. Gilroy, CA: Aladdin, 1995.

Caps for Sale. Esphyr Slobodkina. Addison-Wesley, 1947.

A Dark, Dark Tale. Ruth Brown. New York: Dial, 1981.

The Fat Cat. Jack Kent. New York: Scholastic, 1972.

"The Gingerbread Man."

"Goldilocks and the Three Bears."

Good Night Owl. Pat Hutchins. New York: Macmillan, 1972

"Henny Penny."

"I'm Tipingee, She's Tipingee, We're Tipingee Too." In *The Magic Orange Tree and Other Haitian Folktale*. Diane Wolkstein. Knopf, 1978.

It Could Always Be Worse. Margo Zemach. New York: Farrar, Straus & Giroux, 1977.

The Judge: An Untrue Tale. Harve Zemach. New York: Farrar, Straus & Giroux, 1969.

"Lazy Jack." (See also "Idle Jack.")

The Little Red Hen. Paul Galdone. New York: Seabury, 1973.

Lizard's Song. George Shannon. New York: Greenwillow, 1981.

Magic Wings. Diane Wolkstein. Boston: Little, Brown, 1983

Mama Don't Allow. Thatcher Hurd. Harper, 1985.

The Mitten.

Pierre. Maurice Sendak. Harper, 1962.

Piney Woods Peddler. George Shannon. New York: Greenwillow, 1981.

"Sody Saleratus". *Grandfather Tales.* Richard Chase. Boston: Houghton-Mifflin, 1948.

Tailypo: A Ghost Story. Joanna Galdone. New York: Seabury, 1977.

The Teeny, Tiny Woman: A Ghost Story. Paul Galdone. Boston: Houghton Mifflin, 1982.

"The Three Billy Goats Gruff."

"The Three Little Pigs."

The Turnip. Janina Domanska. New York: Macmillan, 1959.

Where the Wild Things Are .Maurice Sendak. New York: Harper, 1963.

Who's in Rabbit's House?

"Why Dogs Hate Cats." In *The Knee-High Man.* Julius Lester. New York: Dial, 1972.

"The Yellow Ribbon." In *Juba This and Juba That.* Virginia Tashjian. Boston: Little, Brown, 1995.

SONG, MOVEMENT, AND PROPS STORIES

Bay, Jeanette Graham. *Treasury of Flannel Board Stories.* Upstart Library Promotionals, 1995.

Faurot, Kimberly K. *Books in Bloom: Creative Patterns and Props that Bring Stories to Life.* Chicago: ALA Editions, 2003.

Fugita, Hiroko, and Fran Stallings, adapt. and ed. *Kids' Tales: Told with Puppets, paper, Toys and Imagination.* August House, 1999.

Gryski, Camilla. *Cat's Cradle, Owl's Eyes: A Book of String Games.* Scholastic, 1995.

Holt, David. *Folk Rhythms: Learn to Play Spoons, Bones, Washboard, Hambone and the Paper Bag.* Homespun Video, 1995.

Jaffe, Nina. *Patakin! World Tales of Drums and Drummers.* Publishers Group West, 2001. (Reissued in paperback with CD.)

Kallevig, Christine. *Folding Stories: Storytelling and Origami as One.* Storytime Inc. International, 1991.

MacDonald, Margaret Read. *Shake It Up Tales: Stories to Sing, Dance Drum and Act Out.* August House, 2000.

Painter, William H. *Storytelling with Music, Puppets, and Arts for Libraries and Classrooms.* Linnet, 1982.

Pellowski, Anne. *The Family Storytelling Handbook: How to Use Stories, Anecdotes, Rhymes, Handkerchiefs, paper and Other Objects to Enrich Your Family Traditions.* New York: Macmillan, 1987.

WEBLIOGRAPHY FOR STORYTELLING, STORYTELLERS, AND STORIES

www.storyarts.org

Heather Forest, storyteller and musician, created this site. It is attractive, easy to navigate, and useful for teachers and librarianss.

www.twu.edu/cope/slis/storytell.htm

The original, and still the best, online storytelling chat and information-sharing site. Maintained by Texas Women's University library school. Opinionated, sometimes shrill, and wise. Be forewarned: there are dozens of postings.

www.storytellingcenter.net

The site for Storytelling Foundation International that sponsors the annual National Storytelling Festival.

www.storynet.org

The home site for the National Storytelling Network. *The* membership organization for storytellers nationally. Offers the National Storytelling Conference each year.

www.snopes.com

A delicious survey and debunking of urban legends. Easy to pick up good stories, and irresistible to surf through.

www.AesopFables.com/

A really good site, with access to hundreds of Aesop's fables.

www.pitt.edu/~dash/folktexts.html

D. L. Ashliman's essential site provides folk texts, Germanic traditional material, links, and a terrific subject index to tales.

www.pantheon.org

An Internet encyclopedia of myth and folklore; new articles added frequently.

www.afsnet.org/sections/narrative/

The site for the Folk Narrative Section of the American Folklore Society. Includes a bibliography.

Index

About the Authors

Kendall Haven. The only West Point graduate and only senior oceanographer to become a professional storyteller, Haven has performed for four million. He has won numerous awards for his story writing and his storytelling and has conducted story writing and storytelling workshops for 40,000 teachers and librarians and 200,000 students. Haven has published five audiotapes and twenty-five books, including three award-winning books on story: *Write Right* and *Get It Write* on writing, and *Super Simple Storytelling*, on doing, using, and teaching storytelling. Through this work he has become a nationally recognized expert on the architecture of narratives and on teaching creative and expository writing.

Haven served on the National Storytelling Association's Board of Directors and founded the International Whole Language Umbrella's Storytelling Interest Group. He served as co-director of the Sonoma and Bay Area Storytelling Festivals, was an advisor to the Mariposa Storytelling Festival, and is founder of Storytelling Festivals in Las Vegas, Nevada, and Boise, Idaho. He lives with his wife in the rolling Sonoma County grape vineyards in rural Northern California.

Gay Ducey was raised in New Orleans, with its parade of ritual and play, and has been trafficking in stories from the time she was born. She has been a children's librarian for Oakland Public Library for twenty-four years and is the staff trainer for Books for Wider Horizons, a program that sends volunteers into local Head Start centers to present story times. A celebrated storytelling educator, she has taught storytelling in UC Berkeley's graduate division and Dominican University, among others, and has traveled the United States and to Canada and Ireland, telling stories to every age. She has been a commissioned artist at the Smithsonian's Museum of American History and was named an "Outstanding Woman of Berkeley." Ducey is the artistic director of the Bay Area Storytelling Festival. She and her family live in Berkeley.